Flesh of the Church, Flesh of Christ

J.-M.-R. Tillard

Translated by
Madeleine Beaumont

Flesh of the Church, Flesh of Christ

At the Source of the
Ecclesiology of Communion

A PUEBLO BOOK

The Liturgical Press Collegeville, Minnesota

A Pueblo Book published by The Liturgical Press.

Design by Frank Kacmarcik, Obl.S.B. Cover photo courtesy of Robin Pierzina, O.S.B.

This book was originally published in French under the title *Chair de l'Église, chair du Christ: Aux sources de l'ecclésiologie de communion* © 1992 by Les Éditions du Cerf, Paris, France. All rights reserved.

Scripture quotations are from The New Revised Standard Version Bible, Catholic edition, © 1989 by the Division of Christian Education of the National Council of Churches of Christ in the USA. Used by permission. All rights reserved.

Library of Congress Cataloging-in-Publication Data

Tillard, J.-M.-R. (Jean-Marie-Roger), 1927–2000
    [Chair de l'Église, chair du Christ.   English]
    Flesh of the church, flesh of Christ : at the source of the ecclesiology of
Communion / J.-M.-R. Tillard ; translated by Madeleine Beaumont.
      p. cm.
    "A Pueblo book."
    Includes bibliographical references and index.
    ISBN 0-8146-6181-5 (alk. paper).
    1. Church. 2. Church—Unity.   3. Lord's Supper—Catholic Church.
4. Catholic Church—Doctrines.   I. Title.

BX1746.T5213   2000
262'.72—dc21

                                00-058906

Contents

v

1211 04

CONCLUSION

INDEXES

Foreword

A New Ecclesiology?

After the publication of our book *Church of Churches*,[1] we were asked to pursue our reflection by going deeper into what a worried theologian called our undemonstrated "presupposition," liable to become a new "ecumenical dogma." Is it accurate to assert that the idea of *communion* as "flesh of the Church"—to quote one of our images—is a heritage from the first Christian generations, accepted by everyone and faithfully kept down to the great rifts that were to break apart Christendom?

1. We are told that the problem does not reside primarily in the "hierarchical communion" of the various leaders of the church. It is much larger and deeper. Indeed, we affirm that for the common tradition of the first centuries, Christian existence, under all its aspects and in all its components, is integrally a *church* existence. We actually have written that nothing—from the act of faith to the beatific vision, from private prayer to the eternal liturgy described in the book of Revelation, from personal testimony to commitment to the community, from self-respect to defense of the rights of those who are oppressed— escapes the reach of the communion into which baptism introduces us and which the Eucharist seals and signifies. Is this insertion into the ecclesial communion, thus defined as constituting what it means to be a Christian and theologically explained in reference to the Eucharist, in harmony with what the West has always strongly stressed concerning the unique and uncommunicable relation which grace creates be-

[1] Jean-Marie-Roger Tillard, *Church of Churches: The Ecclesiology of Communion,* Collegeville, Minn.: The Liturgical Press, 1992.

tween the individual Christian and God? Is there not a plane—the most profound of Christian experience—which is beyond the reach of the ecclesial, the plane of the most private and personal communion with God? Could it not be said that all the other planes of communion are subordinate to this latter, have meaning only through it, prepare it, and derive from it? Would not the Church be the communion of brothers and sisters helping one another, with the help of the sacraments, to accede to the experience of a wholly private and personal relation to God? Everything would take place *in the Church* but everything would not be *of the Church,* the most important level of the Christian vocation being the sole province of God and the individual soul. Obviously, we are being referred to the testimony of the mystics, which would show that at its finest point the relationship to God transcends the Church. What would then become of our ecclesiology?

2. These questions, put to us by theologians, coincide with practical, or even pastoral, positions. Some spiritual renewals, born of the often grave crises affecting the Christian community, are clearly marked by a rather pietistic approach to the God of faith. Certain currents explicitly tend to place a distance between sacramental life itself and "the communal inflation resulting from Vatican II."[2] There are those who seek a certain elitism, often severe and arrogant with regard to the classical life of the ecclesial community, and prefer belonging to a circle "more given to adoration and more attentive to the message of God's great witnesses, such as the saints and especially the Virgin Mary." These groups foster vocations to ministry and religious life which impart the same orientation to their pastoral and apostolic activity. The local community—with its membership of mediocre, sinful, troubled persons rubbing elbows with the fervent, the devout, and "sincere converts" —does not seem to them to be the place where they belong. It is a place of last resort to which more homogeneous groups are preferred. A young curate formed in a "new community," to whom someone pointed out that the church is precisely this communion of saints and sinners gathered into the body of Christ, had this telling remark, "We must not confuse the house of God with a caravansary."

[2] An important note of the Episcopal Commission on Liturgy and Pastoral Usage of the Sacraments of the Permanent Council of the French Episcopate, on page 5 of its March 1990 report to the Permanent Council stresses "the serious disadvantages deriving from an individualistic conception of the church's sacraments."

In addition, serious studies reveal that a growing number of Catholics, calling themselves practicing Catholics, consider "the eucharistic celebration" with the community "useful but not primary," "enriching but not indispensable."[3] What is more, one sometimes reads disclosures such as this: "If I observe within my circle the law of the gospel according to my conviction; if I pray according to my needs; if, through serious reading, I learn more and more about my faith; if, when I really feel the need of it, I go to the Eucharist where I know it will be celebrated to my taste, I am conscious of having a good relationship with the God of my baptism and that is sufficient for my belonging to the church." Where is communion?

3. All this puts into question the way the tradition of the first centuries understood the link between membership in the Church and the Eucharist. According to this tradition, the Eucharist is not just the "fountain of graces from which one drinks when one is thirsty."[4] It is the sacramental event by which the church "that is in such and such a place" expresses its nature: to be a gathering of human diversity in Christ, who reconciles it with the Father and reconciles its members with one another. Is it possible that this patristic vision—the one which the ecclesiology of communion intends to preserve—is too sacramental? And here, from entirely different quarters, we face the very same question put to us by theologians. Does this ecclesiology really correspond to the conviction manifested from the beginning by the West? Is it not too influenced by the theology of the East? Is it really a common heritage? Would it not be possible to have a less communion-oriented reading of the New Testament? Would not the fact that the Reformation occurred in the West prove that the ethos of the West is more individualistic than communal, more interested in the inner life than in sacraments? Did not John Henry Newman say, "A true Christian, then, may almost be defined as one who has a

---

[3] In the same vein, see the important report (and its commentary) "Les Catholiques crû 90" (Catholics, vintage 1990), *La Vie* 2336 (June 7–13, 1990) in particular pp. 22–24, 29: "92% of Catholics answer, 'One can be a practicing Catholic in different ways and not only by regularly attending Mass.'" See also "Les Catholiques parlent de leur Église," (Catholics speak of their church), *La Vie* 2235 (May 31–June 6, 1990) 21–52.

[4] We found this expression in a leaflet of spirituality quite widespread in French-speaking parishes.

ruling sense of God's presence within him"?[5] And in his well-known meditation on the dialogue between Mary Magdalene and the Risen One, he gave the following description of the life of grace: "inward in presence, and intimate in fruition, a principle of life and a seed of immortality, that thou mayest 'bring forth fruit unto God.'"[6]

4. All these are important questions. We shall not seek to answer them directly. We shall limit ourselves to providing the basis from which the answer must come. Without repeating what we have written elsewhere—which explains the shortness of the first chapter—we shall attempt to define clearly what the flesh of the Church is for the New Testament and what is called the period of the undivided Church. We keep this latter expression, although we know it is inexact because it overlooks the schism of the churches that rejected the Council of Chalcedon in 451. We shall elude the difficulty by citing the Fathers of the Church who lived before this crisis. In any case, this crisis did not greatly affect the conception of the fundamental nature of God's Church that Christians held at that time.

In order to facilitate the reading of this book, we have consented to reduce the notes. The result is that bibliographical references are limited to the strictly necessary and that certain authors who contributed to our reflection on a given point are not mentioned. May the readers forgive us. We also have avoided repeating the abundant bibliographies listed in *Church of Churches*.

5. It seems to us that in its simplicity, this book will enable readers to understand, not the structure of God's Church—this was described in *Church of Churches*—but the living reality of grace for which this structure exists. In effect, it is the second volume of our ecclesiology of communion.

6. We have quoted certain texts in their entirety in order to highlight the context of some of the expressions on which the ecclesiology of communion is based.

---

[5] John Henry Newman, *Parochial and Plain Sermons*, vol. 5 (London: Longmans, Green, 1899) no. 16, p. 225.

[6] John Henry Newman, *Lectures on the Doctrine of Justification*, 3rd ed. (Westminster, Md.: Christian Classics, 1966) no. 9, p. 217.

Abbreviations

Aug. *Misc.* Augustine, Saint, Bishop of Hippo. *Miscellanea agostiniana, testi e studi*. 2 vols. Rome: Tipografia poliglotta vaticana, 1930–31.

Aug. *Œuvres* Augustine, Saint, Bishop of Hippo. *Œuvres de Saint Augustin*. Vols. Bibliothèque augustinienne. Paris: Desclée, De Brouwer, 1936–.

b. Babylonian Talmud

CCL Corpus Christianorum, series Latina. Turnholt: Brepols.

CSEL Corpus Scriptorum Ecclesiasticorum Latinorum. Vienna: [various publishers].

DSp *Dictionnaire de spiritualité: ascétique et mystique, doctrine et histoire*. 17 vols., Marcel Viller, ed. Paris: Beauchesne, 1932–1995.

En in Ps Augustine. *Enarrationes in Psalmos*.

Exp on Ps Augustine. *Expositions on the Psalms*.

Hill Augustine, Saint, Bishop of Hippo. *The Works of Saint Augustine*. Ed. John E. Rotelle. Part 2: *Sermons*. 11 vols. Trans. Edmund Hill. Brooklyn: New City Press, 1990–.

MD *Maison-Dieu*

NRT *Nouvelle revue de théologique*

PG Migne, Jacques-Paul, ed. *Patrologiae cursus completus, series Graeca*, 162 vols. Paris: Migne, 1857–1866.

Philo, *Works* Philo. *The Works of Philo, Complete and Unabridged*. Trans. Charles D. Yonge. 1854–1855. Reprint,

Peabody, Mass: Hendrickson, 1993. [All quotations from this edition have been adapted by the editor.]

PL	____. *Patrologiae cursus completus: series Latina.* 221 vols. Paris: Migne, 1844–1891.
PL-S	Hamman, Adalberto. *Patrologiae cursus completus, series Latina: Supplementum.* 5 vols. Paris: Garnier Freres, 1958–1967.
RB	*Revue biblique*
REA	*Revue des études augustiniennes*
RHE	*Revue d'histoire ecclésiastique*
Roberts	Roberts, Alexander, and James Donaldson, eds. *The Ante-Nicene Fathers.* 10 vols. American reprint, ed. Cleveland Cox. 1885–1897. Reprint, Grand Rapids, Mich.: Eerdmans, 1978–1981. [All quotations from this edition have been adapted by the editor.]
RSPT	*Revue des sciences philosophiques et théologiques*
RSR	*Recherches de sciences religieuses*
SC	Sources Chretiennes. Paris: Cerf.
Schaff	Schaff, Philip, ed. *A Select Library of the Nicene and Post-Nicene Fathers.* 14 vols. 1886–1890. Reprint, Grand Rapids, Mich.: Eerdmans, 1997–1980. [All quotations from this edition have been adapted by the editor.]
Schaff and Wace	Schaff, Philip, and Henry Wace, eds. *A Select Library of the Nicene and Post-Nicene Fathers: Second Series.* 14 vols. 1890–1900. Reprint, Grand Rapids, Mich.: Eerdmans, 1978–1979. [All quotations from this edition have been adapted by the editor.]
ST IIIa	Thomas Aquinas. *The "Summa Theologica" of St. Thomas Aquinas, Part III.* Literally trans. by fathers of the English Dominican Province. No. 3 (qq 50–83). New York: Benziger, 1914. [All quotations from this edition have been adapted by the editor.]

Chapter 1

All Linked Together by Salvation:
For God, in Communion

Whoever reads the New Testament uninterruptedly is struck by the fact that the paraeneses or exhortations, which are a large part of the most important books, insist much more on the glorification of God and the behavior to adopt toward *others* than on an ethics centered on the individual. Of course, duties toward one's body, one's soul, one's possessions are not negated in any way. But they are always inserted into a whole that both goes beyond them and conditions them. Within this whole, God and others are the overall coordinates of Christian life. Christian life is a life in and of the church.

If we needed to characterize in one word the fundamental inspiration of Christian behavior, we would speak of communion—communion with God and others in faith, charity, hope—and not just of a motivation for charity which would be summed up in the will "to do good to others." For, as well as service, this fundamental inspiration equally implies the desire to be *with* others in the common confession of the God and Father of Jesus and in the dynamism of the reign. It is not a mistake to state that when speaking of the formally evangelical life necessarily led *before God*, the other is always in view because of God. And this is so even when Paul deals with a notorious case of incest that occurred in the church of Corinth (1 Cor 5:1-13), with recourse to pagan courts of law (6:1-11), with fornication (6:12-20). On the one hand, *before God*, this relationship with the other goes far beyond action. On the other hand, this relationship has its foundation in the very fact of *being a Christian*. In order to deepen ecclesial life, we think it important to begin by evoking in broad outline the presence of this vision in the major traditions which together form the New Testament. In another chapter, we shall scrutinize in more detail certain aspects of this synthesis.

I. IN CHRIST, IN THE SPIRIT

1. The essential place of the relation to the other in the very essence of being a Christian is evident in Paul. Obviously, here the other immediately suggests Christ Jesus, the object of God's gospel. A sentence from the second letter to the Corinthians perfectly sums up what is found again in other texts: "And he died for all, so that those who live might live no longer for themselves, but for him who died and was raised for them" (5:15).[1] This reference to the person of Christ Jesus, in whom "is fulfilled"[2] the relation of God the Father to humankind, is all-encompassing. For the other that Christ is fundamentally (in his essential reference to the Father) the source of the Christian way of life and its constant support:

"For if while we were enemies, we were reconciled to God through the death of his Son, much more surely, having been reconciled, will we be saved by his life" (Rom 5:10).

"If God is for us, who is against us? He who did not withhold his own Son, but gave him up for all of us, will he not with him also give us everything else? Who will bring any charge against God's elect? It is God who justifies. Who is to condemn? It is Christ Jesus, who died, yes, who was raised, who is at the right hand of God, who indeed intercedes for us. Who will separate us from the love of Christ? . . . For I am convinced that neither death, nor life, nor angels, nor rulers, nor things present, nor things to come, nor powers, nor height, nor depth, nor anything else in all creation, will be able to separate us from the love of God in Christ Jesus our Lord" (Rom 8:31-39).

The whole of Christian life is lived in communion with the other; now, Christ is the other to such an extent that Christian life can be described as the life of Christ himself in the believer:

"I have been crucified with Christ; and it is no longer I who live, but it is Christ who lives in me. And the life I now live in the flesh I live by

---

[1] See Charles Kingsley Barrett, *The Second Epistle to the Corinthians* (Harper and Row: New York, 1973) 169: "Because Christ, being the person he was, died and was raised, there exists the universal possibility *(he died in behalf of all; all died)* of a new kind of human existence, no longer centred upon self, but centred upon Christ."

[2] With the full meaning of *teleiōsis,* that is, the point at which a plan, nurtured for a long time, reaches its realization; Ephesians calls it "the mystery of his will" (Eph 1:9; see Rom 16:25; Col 2:2-3).

faith in the Son of God, who loved me and gave himself for me" (Gal 2:19-20; see Gal 6:17; 2 Cor 4:10; Phil 1:21; Col 1:24; 3:3).

Nothing in the life of a Christian escapes this hold Christ has: Christ lives in the believer, the believer lives in Christ; Christ—always understood in his union with his God and Father—is the one *for* whom the believer lives (2 Cor 5:15; see Rom 6:11; Gal 2:19), the believer is the one *for* whom Christ died. It is therefore possible to say that life "in Christ" *(en Christō)* defines the Christian way of life. As chapter 8 of the Letter to the Romans emphasizes, the paradox is precisely that it is only by allowing oneself to be possessed by Christ (and endued with life by the Spirit) that the believer comes to know authentic freedom, that of the adopted children of the Father *in the Son*, freedom which is salvation. It is not by chance that the locution *en Christō* occurs 164 times in the Pauline corpus alone; it is in all the letters except Titus.[3] It is the specific indicator of the communion with God established by the salvific death and resurrection of the Lord Jesus Christ. In this perspective, the full weight of Paul's confession is obvious: "God is faithful; by him you were called into the fellowship *[koinōnia]* of his Son, Jesus Christ the Lord" (1 Cor 1:9). It is in this that salvation resides and gives the Christian condition its specific stamp.

At its source, the Christian way of life is radically, in virtue of God's very self, the absolute negation of any form of self-sufficiency, of any sort of self-absorption. The relationship to the other—this other who is first of all God, but God grasped within the unity between brothers and sisters in Christ Jesus—is intrinsic to the Christian way of life. It constitutes it.[4] Where the communion of Christ Jesus is not present, the Christian way of being is absent. What we are speaking about is communion (1 Cor 1:9), not absorption, because freedom is at the very

[3] A list of Paul's texts in which the formula *en Christō* is used, together with a classification, can be found in Fernand Prat, *La Théologie de saint Paul*, 3rd ed., vol. 1 (1909) 434–35, and their analysis, 424–25; [Fernand Prat, *The Theology of St. Paul*, 11th ed., 2 vols. in 1, trans. John L. Stoddard (London: Burns and Oates, 1964)]. On this question, see Michel Bouttier, *En Christ: Études d'exégèse et de théologie pauliniennes*, Études d'histoire et de philosophie religieuses 54 (Paris, Presses universitaires de France, 1962); [Michel Bouttier, *Christianity according to Paul*, trans. Frank Clarke, Biblical Theology 49 (Naperville, Ill.: Allenson, 1966)].

[4] See Lucien Cerfaux, *La Théologie de l'Église suivant saint Paul* (Paris: Cerf, 1974) 122. See especially Jerome Murphy-O'Connor, *L'Existence chrétienne selon saint Paul* (Paris: Cerf, 1974) 77–88; Ralph P. Martin, *The Spirit and the Congregation: Studies in 1 Corinthians 12–15* (Grand Rapids, Mich.: Eerdmans, 1984).

core of this process of salvation. But this relation to Christ is inseparable from the relation to others. The other implies others.

2. The attentive study of the uses of *en Christō* in the Pauline corpus
reveals other very important points. First of all, more than exegetes
are wont to do, we must place two remarks side by side: first, the
wording "in Jesus" is never used, but the expression "in Christ Jesus"
is; second, the expression *en Christō* is closely related to the expression
en pneumati ("in the Spirit"). It is true that today the thesis of the practical equivalence of the two expressions is criticized.[5] However, it is
important to perceive clearly how "in Christ" and "in the Spirit" call
for one another. Believers cannot be "in Christ" without being "in the
Spirit." Because if it is true that Christ gives the Spirit (Gal 3:13-14),[6] it
is equally true that the Spirit is closely associated with the Lord's
resurrection (Rom 1:4; 8:11) and that it is through the Spirit that Christians are enabled to be "in Christ." Indeed, it is from the Spirit that
faith is born (1 Cor 12:3; see Gal 3:2); it is from the Spirit that life according to God proceeds with its whole retinue of virtues (Gal 5:16-25;
Rom 14:17); it is in the Spirit that the power of the gospel rests (1 Thess
1:5); it is from the Spirit that the gifts fostering life in individuals and
communities derive (1 Cor 12:4-30; 14:1); it is from the Spirit that
prayer wells up (Rom 8:15-16; Gal 4:6); it is in the Spirit that we have
an intercessor with God (Rom 8:27); it is in the Spirit that the freedom
of God's children originates (Rom 8:12-16); it is from the Spirit that the
resurrection will come (Rom 8:11); it is through the Spirit that the
adoption of human beings as God's children is effected (Rom 8:15).
For Paul and the author of the Acts of the Apostles, this Spirit is the
eschatological Spirit that has the power to call God's world into existence: the world which is expected and of which the Spirit already
gives the first installment (2 Cor 1:22; 5:5) or, in another text, the firstfruits (Rom 8:23).[7]

[5] As is well known, this is the position of Gustav Adolf Deissmann, *Die neutesta-
mentliche Formel in Christo Jesu* (Marburg: Elwert, 1892). It has been criticized by
Ernst Percy, *Der Leib Christi (sōma Christou) in den paulinischen Homologoumena und
Antilegomena* (Lund: Gleerup, 1942).

[6] Which is less clear in Paul than in the Acts.

[7] See Ernst Käsemann, *Commentary on Romans,* trans. and ed. Geoffrey W.
Bromiley (Grand Rapids, Mich.: Eerdmans, 1980) 237–39: "The apostle passionately
longs for the liberation of existence from temptation and decay in favor of a mode
of being in a world that belongs to God alone."

It is significant that Paul only rarely uses the titles Spirit of Christ (as in Rom 8:9) or Spirit of the Son (as in Gal 4:6). He ordinarily says Spirit of God, *pneuma tou Theou*, (thus in Rom 8:9, 11, 14; 15:19; 1 Cor 1:11, 12, 14; 3:16; 6:11; 7:48; 12:3; 2 Cor 3:3). The meaning is clear. Because the unique and indivisible Spirit dwells both in Christ, the new Adam, and in all believers, the adopted children, God in person makes of all these a communion of the children of God in the "Spirit of God" (see 2 Cor 13:13): the communion of the children of God all gathered "in Christ" as *filii in Filio* (sons and daughters in the Son).[8] Thus, they are saved because they are at peace with God. They are saved through the work of Christ: "in Christ God was reconciling the world to himself" (2 Cor 5:19). However, it is the Spirit of God which is the agent of this communion in Christ, who is the Son. "In Christ" and "in the Spirit" are inseparable, like the two faces of God's intervention in salvation:

"You have received a spirit of adoption. When we cry, Abba! Father! it is that very Spirit bearing witness with our spirit that we are children of God" (Rom 8:15-16; see Rom 8:9-14).

The letter to the Galatians could not be any clearer:

"God sent his Son, born of a woman, born under the law, in order . . . that we might receive adoption as children. And because you are children, God has sent the Spirit of his Son into our hearts, crying, 'Abba! Father!' So you are no longer a slave but a child, and if a child then also an heir, through God" (4:4-7).

Irenaeus will say that the Son and the Spirit are the two hands of God.

3. To characterize the communion in this unity of life which comes from the Spirit given by Christ—who at the resurrection and through the Spirit became the spiritual Adam, the source of new life (1 Cor 15:46, *ho eschatos Adam eis pneuma zōopoioun*)—Paul coins an expression, body of Christ:

"For in one Spirit we were all baptized into one body—Jews or Greeks, slaves or free—and we were all made to drink of one Spirit" (1 Cor 12:13).

[8] See the classic study of Emile Mersch, "Filii in Filio," *NRT* 65 (1938) 551–82, 681–702, 809–30.

To be included in salvation is to be in Christ, the new Adam. Furthermore, to be "in Christ" is to find oneself under the power of the Spirit *of God* that, being inseparable from the work of Jesus, Son *of God*, knits into the unity of one body those who receive the gospel *of God*. Thus is constituted the church *of God*, explicitly evoked in this context (1 Cor 12:27-28). Soon afterward, in the same Pauline tradition, the letter to the Colossians and the letter to the Ephesians will simply identify the church with the body of Christ, "the body, the church" (Col 1:18-19; Eph 1:22-23). Therefore, to receive salvation from God is to be inserted into a body animated by the Spirit of God, the body of Christ, the church.

This statement implies that reconciliation with God is inseparable from entrance into the unity of sisters and brothers in the body of Christ. Belonging to the union between sisters and brothers in the ecclesial body is part of the new economy created by salvation. Whoever is "in Christ" and "in the Spirit" never is in a relation of one to one with God. Because life "in Christ" implies not only the other that Christ Jesus is, and under whose sway one lives, but also others, the members of the body of Christ to which one is not added but "associated" in the same way, Paul explains, as the eye is associated with the hand, the weaker members with the stronger ones, so that "if one member suffers, all suffer together with it" (1 Cor 12:26). The life that is reconciled with God is led with others, and this by its very nature. It is not only a life *in the church* but—the nuance is of crucial importance —a life *from and by the church*.

Obviously, the life of the body is expressed in solidarity. But this does not have the others for its sole object. It is true that in a lengthy and marvelous development, Romans rereads the gospel law in terms of solidarity between brothers and sisters and of communion in mutual service:

"For as in one body we have many members, and not all the members have the same function, so we, who are many, are one body in Christ, and individually we are members one of another. We have gifts that differ according to the grace given to us; prophecy, in proportion to faith; ministry, in ministering; the teacher, in teaching; the exhorter, in exhortation; the giver, in generosity; the leader, in diligence; the compassionate, in cheerfulness.

"Let love be genuine; hate what is evil, hold fast to what is good; love one another with mutual affection; outdo one another in showing honor. Do not lag in zeal, be ardent in spirit, serve the Lord. . . . Contribute to the needs of saints; extend hospitality to strangers.

"Bless those who persecute you; bless and do not curse them. Rejoice with those who rejoice, weep with those who weep. Live in harmony with one another. . . . Do not repay anyone evil for evil, but take thought for what is noble in the sight of all. If it is possible, so far as it depends on you, live peaceably with all. Beloved, never avenge yourselves, but leave room for the wrath of God; for it is written, 'Vengeance is mine, I will repay, says the Lord.' No, 'if your enemies are hungry, feed them; if they are thirsty, give them something to drink; for by doing this you will heap burning coals on their heads.' Do not be overcome by evil, but overcome evil with good" (Rom 12:4-21).

Further on, Paul reminds his readers that charity is the fullness of the Law (13:10) and gives the norms of personal behavior (13:13-14); then he comes back at length to relationships between brothers and sisters, especially with regard to the weaker members. And he sees in this the very substance of a "spiritual worship" (12:1) where God is glorified in the communion of brothers and sisters:

"May the God of steadfastness and encouragement grant you to live in harmony with one another, in accordance with Christ Jesus, so that together you may with one voice glorify the God and Father of our Lord Jesus Christ" (15:5-6).

Because of what God has accomplished "in Christ," the glorification of God is itself channelled by the communion of the ecclesial body. The Letter to the Philippians will say this in lyrical terms (Phil 2:1-11).

4. If things are so, one is able to understand better why it is Ephesians—no doubt rooted in the Pauline tradition but exhibiting traits peculiar to itself suggesting a hand different from Paul's—which favors the expression "in Christ" (used in thirty-five undeniable instances) and gives it its full force.[9] Indeed, the author of this letter places at the core of faith the abolition of division through the cross on which

[9] See Jean-Marie-Roger Tillard, *Church of Churches: The Ecclesiology of Communion* (Collegeville, Minn.: The Liturgical Press, 1992), in which we have studied at length the ecclesiology of this letter. We also gave an extensive bibliography in the same book.

Christ killed hatred. He exalts the resulting unity *in him* whom the Father established at the resurrection as head of the church (2:13-22). The reality of the one and only body, with its one and only Spirit (4:4) and its origin in the destruction, through the cross, of the walls of separation, gives Christian life its fundamental law. And this law is "to imitate God" by living "in love as *[kathōs]* Christ loved us and gave himself up for us" (Eph 5:1-2). Such a demand is put into practice within a whole network of behaviors whose norm is usually reference to others. What is at stake is building the body of Christ in unity according to the "new self" (Eph 4:24). For the new self, faithfulness to God is never separated from Christ Jesus, whose life and work were centered, not on his own person, but inseparably on God (the Father) and others. Even more than in the paraenesis of Romans, here others are always in the believer's line of vision.

"So then, putting away falsehood, let all of us speak the truth to our neighbors, for we are members of one another. Be angry but do not sin; do not let the sun go down on your anger, and do not make room for the devil. Thieves must give up stealing; rather let them labor and work honestly with their own hands, so as to have something to share with the needy. Let no evil talk come out of your mouths, but only what is useful for building up, as there is need, so that your words may give grace to those who hear. And do not grieve the Holy Spirit of God, with which you were marked with a seal for the day of redemption. Put away from you all bitterness and wrath and anger and wrangling and slander, together with all malice, and be kind to one another, tenderhearted, forgiving one another, as God in Christ has forgiven you. Therefore be imitators of Christ, as beloved children, and live in love, as Christ loved us and gave himself up for us, a fragrant offering and sacrifice to God" (Eph 4:25–5:2).

This is applied even to prayer: "sing . . . among yourselves" (5:18-20).

In its dynamism, springing from the one Spirit, the "new life" is characterized by a trait inherited from Christ's behavior toward the body whose savior he is by delivering himself up for it (5:23-30): "Be subject to one another" (5:21). One lives "in Christ" by being made, in one's daily conduct, like to the Lord Jesus through the Spirit. It is thus that the church *is* the body of Christ, not in virtue of a purely juridical or abstract identification, but *in virtue of its very life*. It is Christ imprinting his own life in the life of his body and, together with his life, imprinting his relationship with the Father whom he glorifies in this body.

The equivalence "flesh of the church"—"flesh of Christ" comes from Ephesians. The Church-Bride is presented as the very flesh of Christ-Bridegroom (5:27-32), his own body. In addition, some manuscripts, inspired by Genesis 2:21-23, add the gloss "taken from his own flesh and his own bones," therefore, "one flesh with him." However, we must note that the author of Ephesians speaks of the whole body in its relation both to its head (5:23) and to its members:

"For no one ever hates his own body, but he nourishes it and tenderly cares for it, just as Christ does for the church, because we are members of his body. For this reason a man will leave his father and mother and be joined to his wife, and the two will become one flesh. This is a great mystery, and I am applying it to Christ and the church" (5:29-32).[10]

One single body, with several members, all as different as the eye is from the ear, the foot from the heart, such is the status of the church of God. These members are different. The fact that everything is "of the church" does not mean that everything is uniform, reduced to one expression and one opinion. Both individuals and local churches are led by the Spirit to a deepening and acknowledgement of their specific characters which are thus made into an asset for the church. It is important to stress this fact.

Indeed, difference is intrinsic to the communion which constitutes the church; difference is one of the components of this communion. The church is neither abolition nor addition but communion of "differences." Abolition levels everything to a single feature. Addition does not necessarily presuppose that the elements are assembled in view of the common good: an addition is a sum of individuals. On the contrary, communion demands that a common reality, a unique value be present in all members and that all have part in it, albeit in very diverse ways. There is a radical unity on which their difference flourishes. By simply adding up differences, one creates a crowd. By causing the common reality hidden under differences to emerge, one manifests a communion, one reveals the riches of unity, one acknowledges the nobility of difference.

[10] See Markus Barth, *Ephesians, 4–6,* Anchor Bible 34A (Garden City, N.Y.: Doubleday, 1974), 632–47.

As a consequence, difference has a special role in ecclesiology. This is true at the level of each community and at the level of the communion of all the churches. Although Ephesians does not apply the idea of body to the communion of local churches in their diversity, but only to the communion of the members, tradition will come through deduction to the logical conclusion that the local churches are also in communion.

Therefore, in accordance with the logic of the law of incarnation, the communion of each local church—and that of the local churches among themselves—corresponds to the variety of creation and the twists and turns of history. Communion is not a vague reality ignoring the riches of the natural solidarities which are one of the gifts of humanity. These are part of the realities which grace assumes, preserves, promotes by making of them an heirloom of the catholic world. The church is catholic by uniting within the communion of Christ Jesus, which integrates the diversities (having their source in creation) into the space of salvation and the new creation opened by the cross. The church is a communion of churches, themselves made of communions of persons enriching one another through diversity. The New Testament already takes the defense of diversity. The ecclesial status of difference is therefore a favorable one. Under all its forms, it is a rich resource in which the catholic world is embodied. One of the major advances of ecclesiology in the last decades is to have restored to difference its rightful place at the heart of the mystery of the church. Faith does not express itself in the same way in Alexandria and Antioch. Liturgy does not have the same form in Rome and Kinshasa. Bernard does not think like Abelard, Ratramnus like Radbertus, Thomas Aquinas like Bonaventure, Flannery O'Connor like Rosemary Radford Ruether. A Christian from New York does not react like a Christian from Moscow. Freedom of thought, which the experience of the gospel endorses, and the responsibility of each person challenged by the Spirit have free play. Without the specific contribution of each person and each local church, communion fails to thrive. Every person receives the Spirit and transmits it with his or her own breath.

At the same time, individual members of Christ or a local church should not be completely engrossed in what makes them different, by seeing in this difference the essential part of their Christian experience. Besides, the grace which makes them what they are is the grace which brings them into active solidarity with the other members of the body of Christ and, for the local church, with the other churches of God. By virtue of its origin in the paschal assembly gathered by Christ, the church refuses to see its fabric shredded. It rejects the confusion between affirmation of difference and independence. This is why the ecclesiology of communion emphasizes the radical primacy of the gifts of grace held in common and transcending all manner of particularism. They are, as it were, the substance to which the differences give a distinct color. Moreover, this ecclesiology holds that every local church must always be critical of its difference and judge it in reference to those values that are held in common. But upholding the latter allows for the vigorous affirmation of the former. Indeed the more the common ground is firm and deep, the more the differences have space to play and the freedom necessary for their full expression. Provided common absolutes are guaranteed and their validity is not put into question, any community with its particular forms, its singular historical incarnations, even its idiosyncratic objectives and interests can readily recognize that similar things have the right to exist in any other community, each recognizing itself in the other.

Paradoxically, for a Christian to cling tenaciously to one's difference, to the point of seeing nothing else, amounts to excluding oneself from the body, the vine, the dwelling of God; for a local church, it amounts to refusing the possibility of being anything but a sect and of being what it is, in its specificity, within the church. On the contrary, to live one's difference in communion results in giving it full rein, in *agapē*. Again, we encounter what seems to us an evident principle of the gospel: the relation to the other allows even the difference to find its fulfillment. The other has authority over me, but this authority preserves my own self, in communion. It does not smother it, it does not diminish it; it sets it off. What is applied to the member of the body, according to the explicit trend of thought in Ephesians, is applicable also to the local church within the communion of all the churches of God.

5. If, therefore, it is true that in the incontrovertibly authentic letters of Paul and the other documents which are part of the Pauline corpus, the new way of life exists in the space opened by Christ on the cross,[11] we must add that this space is the ecclesial body. The Christian way of life is a way of life in solidarity. Others are essential to it not simply because, by going toward others, believers exercise

[11] According to the fine expression of Heinrich Schlier, *Le Temps de l'Église*, trans. Françoise Corin, Cahiers de l'actualité religieuse 14 (Tournai: Casterman, 1961).

their generosity or augment their merit. Others are radically essential because life "in Christ" is that of a body, the body of reconciled human-kind vivified by the Spirit of the living God. Of course, the faithful fully live this life in their personal destiny. They do not disappear into a great mass. They remain the object of God's love concerning their person, their needs, their own resurrection. Paul is able to write, "[He] loved me and gave himself for me" (Gal 2:20). This was commented upon by Pascal in a short sentence which has given back hope and courage to thousands of believers: "I have sweated such drops of blood for thee."[12] What is more, in prayer and the privacy of their inner selves, believers are urged to establish with God personal rela-tionships of communion, whose depth Philippians suggests (Phil 3:7-16, 20-21). However, life "in Christ" is not restricted to individual believers; it is not their personal possession, even in the case of the most intimate prayer when they are alone before God. A body—the ecclesial body of Christ is no exception—is not the sum of autonomous members. Believers who, like Paul, enter into mystical communion with God always do so as members of the body of Christ.

6. The solidarity of the new life is first actualized in the local commu-nity. But already the letters to the Corinthians widen the perspective:

"Paul . . . [t]o the church *of God* that is in Corinth, to those who are sanctified in Christ Jesus, called to be saints *with all those who in every place call on* the name of our Lord Jesus Christ, both their Lord and ours:
Grace to you and peace *from God our Father* and the Lord Jesus Christ" (1 Cor 1:1-3).[13]

The relationship of the individual to the local community must take place within a similar relationship of the local church to the communi-ties far away. Acts already showed this with regard to material aid. And it is enlightening to read in parallel fashion Acts 4:32-35 and 11:27-30. In 2 Corinthians, Paul knows how to outline the amplitude of the communion which defines the essence of Christian life and con-cerns at once God and others. It does away with the limits imposed by space:

<hr />

[12] Blaise Pascal, *Pensées* no. 552, "The Mystery of Jesus," in *Pascal's Pensées*, trans. William F. Trotter (1923; reprint, New York: Dutton, 1958) 149.

[13] Here and everywhere else throughout this book, the emphases are ours.

"You will be enriched in every way for your great generosity [to other churches], which will produce thanksgiving to God through us; for the rendering of this ministry not only supplies the needs of the saints but also overflows with many thanksgivings to God. Through the testing of this ministry you glorify God by your obedience to the confession of the gospel of Christ and by the generosity of your sharing with them and with all others, while they long for you and pray for you because of the surpassing grace of God that he has given you. Thanks be to God for his indescribable gift" (2 Cor 9:11-15).

This gift is precisely new life, in salvation. Through their generosity, the wealthier churches manifest by their actions the authenticity of this new life *before God*, whom they glorify. For Paul, the church of God is not a collection of autonomous churches, their coexistence simply neighborliness. It is the communion of these churches. Later on, Ephesians will say of the church *as such* that it is the body of Christ, a body made up of members united among themselves and, likewise, of communities united among themselves.

II. THE BRANCHES OF THE VINE

What Paul and Ephesians express by the analogy of the living human body, the Johannine tradition shows by the analogy of the living vine. This analogy has a long past, preserved in the memory of the people of God (thus Isa 5:1-7; 27:2-3; Jer 2:21; 12:10; Ezek 15:1-8; 17:6; 19:10-14; Ps 79:9-17; Cant 1:5-9). It speaks both of God's profound attachment to God's people and of the vitality that the people should draw from it since it is a plant of "truth" (*zera emeth* says Jeremiah in 2:21, "true vine"). John's Gospel identifies this vine with Jesus, understood in his relation to the Father, who is the vinegrower (*geōrgos*, 15:1) caring for his vine and causing it to grow, an idea known to the Pauline tradition (see 1 Cor 3:6-9). The vine—which is Jesus—is made up of branches into which the sap ascends from the roots and promotes the bearing of fruit. The branches are the disciples (15:5).[14]

[14] On John 15, see Annie Jaubert, "L'Image de la vigne," in *Oikonomia: Heilsgeschichte als Thema der Theologie O. Cullmann zum 65 geburtstag gewidmet*, ed. Felix Christ (Hamburg: Reich, 1967) 93–96; Frederick F. Bruce, *Commentary on the Gospel of John* (Grand Rapids, Mich.: Eerdmans, 1983) 309–15; Raymond E. Brown, *The Gospel according to John, 13–21*, Anchor Bible 29A (Garden City, N.Y.: Doubleday, 1970) 658–84; François-Marie Braun, *Jean le Théologien et son Évangile dans l'Église ancienne*, Études bibliques (Paris: Gabalda, 1972) 30–33; Édouard Delebecque,

The attentive study of John 15 reveals several points which are essential for ecclesiological reflection. First of all, as commentators never tire of stressing, the branches are *in* the vine, the disciples *in* Jesus; the vine is *in* the branches, Jesus *in* the disciples (15:4, 5, 6, 7, 8, 10). Thus, Jesus *fulfills* what the image of the vine, essentially collective, meant in the memory of God's people. Obviously, he fulfills it in his own person. His person does not vanish to make room for a mystical collective entity in which he would lose his own attributes and in particular his transcendence in relation to others. It is to himself, in his own "I," that Jesus constantly links what he says of discipleship. This "I" includes in particular his unique and unchangeable relationship with the Father. Moreover, it is he, in his own person, who is the realization of Israel's hope. Nevertheless, between him and his disciples, there exists a bond of reciprocal inclusion. John describes it through the idea of "abode": Jesus declares to his followers that he abides in them and they abide in him (15:4, 5).[15] Hence, they are now one living reality. Furthermore, the union resulting from this "abiding" is so intimate that it can be understood only in reference *(kathōs)* to the bond of *agapē* existing between Jesus and the Father, between the Father and Jesus (15:9-10), just as the unity of the Father and the Son can be glimpsed only through the experience of the bond joining Jesus and the disciples (10:30-38; 17:11, 21, 25).

The unity of the disciples among themselves flows from this mutual abiding. In the vine, all the branches share, by their very nature as branches, the same life which is that of the vine. And if one branch is cut off from the vine, it dies (15:6). It is alive and bears fruit only *in* the vine, that is, in the unity of the vine. Without this living unity, there is only sterility. The same is true of the disciples. Outside the vine whose branches are the other disciples, they no longer bear the fruit that the Father expects, the fruit produced by the union of Jesus and the disciples, the fruit of the vine.

It is evident that the allegory of the vine sheds light on the "that they may be one" of chapter 17. It sheds light especially on the ecclesiological meaning of the precept of charity between sisters and brothers to which it leads. The command, "love one another as *[kathōs]*

Évangile de Jean, texte traduit et annoté, Cahiers de la revue biblique 23 (Paris: Gabalda, 1987) 190–92. On the meaning of *kathōs,* see Olivier de Dinechin, "Kathōs, la similitude dans l'évangile selon Jean," *RSR* 58 (1970) 195–236, especially 208–13.

[15] We have counted fifteen occurrences of the expression "abide in" in John 15.

I have loved you" (15:12) should not be seen as an additional obligation, a precept added to the law ruling Christian living. Rather, without it, there would no longer be any vine but only a bundle of sterile
branches devoid of sap. Not to love the other disciples is, in fact, to
stand outside the *agapē* of the Father and the Son, in which one must
abide if one wants to be a disciple. "If you keep my commandments,
you will abide in my love, just as *[kathōs]* I have kept my Father's
commandments and abide in his love" (15:10). Without love for sisters
and brothers, one separates oneself from the vine. Then one is cut off
from both Jesus and others.

In another context, that of abiding, the First Letter of John will
describe more precisely the nature of this separation.

"We know that we have passed from death to life because we love one
another. Whoever does not love abides in death. . . . We know love
by this, that he laid down his life for us—and we ought to lay down
our lives for one another. How does God's love abide in anyone who
has the world's goods and sees a brother or sister in need and yet
refuses help?

"Little children, let us love, not in speech, but in truth and action. . . .

"And this is his commandment, that we should believe in the name
of his Son Jesus Christ and love one another, just as he has commanded
us. All who obey his commandments abide in him, and he abides in
them. And by this we know that he abides in us, by the Spirit that he
has given us" (1 John 3:14-24).

This gift is that of an anointing *(chrisma)* which abides in believers so
that they remain in the truth of Christ (1 John 2:27), the truth of his
word but also of his *agapē*.

The Johannine tradition is firm and constant in its vision: abiding in
Jesus, which is the very definition of the Christian way of life, necessarily implies a living and concrete relationship with others, branches
of the one vine which Jesus constitutes *with* and *in* his own in a reciprocal interiority or inclusion. The relationship with Jesus is never a
relationship with an isolated Jesus, shut in within the boundaries of
his transcendence. The disciple always joins him in his own relationship with his Father and with those whom the gospel calls his friends
(John 15:14-15). The sap that gives life to each disciple is the *agapē* of
Jesus, but inasmuch as it springs forth from the *agapē* of the Father and
gathers all those whom he, Jesus, makes "his own." The love for

brothers and sisters enjoined on the disciples is nothing else than the *agapē* of Jesus—"laying down his life for his friends" (see 15:13),[16] in total communion with the *agapē* of the Father (3:16; 1 John 4:9)—impregnating their actions and especially the deep motivation of their lives. This love for brothers and sisters is therefore at once what confers on the "friends" of Jesus their new life and what enables them to put this new life into practice: "We know that we have passed from death to life because we love one another. Whoever does not love abides in death" (1 John 3:14).

Chapter 15 of John's Gospel ends with the promise of the coming of the Spirit of truth, the Advocate sent "from the Father" (15:26-27). Speaking of this Spirit of truth, Jesus says: "He will take what is mine and declare it to you. All that the Father has is mine. For this reason I said that he will take what is mine and declare it to you" (16:14-15). What is meant is not only the action that guides disciples "into all the truth" (16:13). What is announced is also the "communication" of the good possessed by Jesus, his *agapē* in which we must abide; where the Spirit of truth "abides" (14:17), there is *agapē* (14:17-23). Consequently, from the Spirit that gives them a new birth (3:5-8), the disciples receive the very power of new life, that of this *agapē* which makes of them, not an armful of cut branches, but one plant, one vine whose many branches are united by the same sap and destined to bear the same fruit. Without the Spirit, the vine dries up and dies.

The Father's glory is also closely linked to the health of the vine. God expects it to produce fruit: "My Father is glorified by this, that you bear much fruit and become my disciples" (15:8). Because the Father is glorified in the Son (14:13), the Father is glorified when *agapē* thrives in the branches. This is the real and full meaning of chapter 17. It is a hymn to the glorification of the Father through the unity of the disciples: "they are yours . . . protect them . . . I have been glorified in them . . . that they may have my joy complete in themselves . . . may they also be [one] in us, so that the world may believe that you have sent me . . . that they may become completely one so that the world may know that you have sent me and have loved them even as you have loved me."

---

[16] Claude Tresmontant, *Évangile de Jean* (Paris: OEIL, 1984) 402–3, proposes to translate, "placing his soul in the palm of his hand" (for those he loves).

III. BOUND WITH ONE ANOTHER,
ONE SINGLE COMMUNITY

1. Ecclesiologists have ordinarily studied only part of the First Letter of Peter and some verses of the Letter of James, isolated from their context. But to us, the block of the catholic epistles seems much more important for a serious reflection on the reality of the church than is sometimes insinuated. This importance is due to the fact that these letters are concerned especially with the life of the Christian community, here and now, challenged by the demands of its faith in a world that contests it.[17] But an exhaustive study quickly reveals that James, Peter, and Jude present what can be called the fundamental law of the life of sisters and brothers which is the life of Christ in God's church. (The Johannine letters belong to another ensemble).

2. James is the most significant for our topic. We insist on it because, written without a clear plan and striking the reader as a chain of poorly connected sentences, it is received as a Christian piece of writing—and not as a Jewish document hastily christianized[18]—offering the author's spontaneous vision of the life of faith. Although the name of the Lord Jesus Christ is mentioned only twice (1:1; 2:1; see 5:14-15), this letter is charged with a precise conception of the life of the church.

The writer, who hides under the name of James (seeking the patronage of the Lord's brother), "speaks with personal warmth of what he considers just, and denounces with prophetic force what he considers unjust. His message is rooted in the conviction that real ailments undermine the life of the young church and that radical remedies are necessary."[19] Everything centers on what threatens the necessary openness to others, the law of the gospel. To state that the "works," whose necessity is underscored, are above all the acts of the authentic Christian relationship with others (which includes more than the sharing of the necessities of life) is not to distort the meaning of the second chapter of this letter—as is confirmed by the explicit example of the prostitute Rahab. From the outset, the letter repeats the teaching of the

---

[17] See Bo Reicke, *The Epistles of James, Peter and Jude*, Anchor Bible 37 (Garden City, N.Y.: 1964) Introduction, xxxvi–xxvii; Peter H. Davids, *The Epistle of James: A Commentary on the Greek Text* (Grand Rapids, Mich.: Eerdmans, 1982).

[18] Reicke, *Epistles*, 8–10, thinks this is the last picture of the Palestinian Church before the wars which will sweep it away.

[19] Ibid. 10.

prophetic tradition: "Religion that is pure and undefiled before God, the Father, is this: to care for orphans and widows in their distress, and to keep oneself unstained by the world" (1:27); this is not simply an accidental remark. One must emphasize this in order to give its true dimension to this question of "works," a source of polemics.

The rest of the letter remains in the same vein, whether the topic is respect for the poor, who must not be "dishonored" (2:6), or more generally "the royal law according to the scripture, 'You shall love your neighbor as yourself'" (2:8). The example given to demonstrate the importance of works is none other than the following:

"If a brother or sister is naked and lacks daily food, and one of you says to them, 'Go in peace; keep warm and eat your fill,' and yet you do not supply their bodily needs, what is the good of that? So faith by itself, if it has no works, is dead" (2:16-17).[20]

If it is true that the context is that of a liturgical assembly, as exegetes think it is[21]—because of the first verses of the chapter ("into your assembly") and the formula "go in peace" (which from the earliest times the deacon proclaimed to conclude the liturgy)—the insistence on others is all the more significant. Confession of faith, liturgical worship, and concrete concern about others necessarily go together: "For just as the body without the spirit is dead, so faith without works is also dead" (2:26; see 2:17, 20, 24). In accordance with the nature of faith, these works concretize the relationship with others which the gospel demands.

James condemns the hearts filled with "bitter envy and selfish ambition," always ready to resort to lying (3:14-18; see 3:5-11). In a long exhortation, it goes on to denounce the source of the disputes and conflicts that wound humankind. In 4:8, it names this source: the double-minded state of the heart *(dipsychia)*. Indeed, torn between obedience to God and love of the world that makes one a slave, one engages in battling others (4:1-12) or one adopts the mores of the world. But by attacking others and judging them, speaking all manner of evil against them, one forgets that the God-given law is found precisely in others:

---

[20] Davids, *Epistle of James,* 122, comments, "Works are not an 'added extra' any more than breath is an 'added extra' to a living body."

[21] Thus Reicke, *Epistles,* 32–35.

"Whoever speaks evil against another or judges another, speaks evil against the law and judges the law; but if you judge the law, you are not a doer of the law but a judge. There is one lawgiver and judge who is able to save and to destroy. So, who then, are you to judge your neighbor?" (4:11-12)

This is verified in particular in the attitude of the rich. Drawing on the sources of the Law and the Prophets,[22] the author castigates those who, eaten up by love of the riches of which they boast, become richer, especially by oppressing and despoiling the poor:

"Come now, you who say, 'Today or tomorrow we shall go to such and such a town and spend a year there, doing business and making money.' Yet you do not even know what tomorrow will bring. What is your life? For you are a mist that appears for a little while and then vanishes. . . .

"Come now, you rich people, weep and wail for the miseries that are coming to you. Your riches have rotted, and your clothes are moth-eaten. Your gold and silver have rusted, and their rust will be evidence against you, and it will eat your flesh like fire. You have laid up treasure for the last days. Listen! The wages of the laborers who mowed your fields, which you kept back by fraud, cry out, and the cries of the harvesters have reached the ears of the Lord of hosts. You have lived on the earth in luxury and in pleasure; you have fattened your heart in a day of slaughter. You have condemned and murdered the righteous one, who does not resist you" (4:13–5:6).

The letter ends with a vivid evocation of the communal dimension of the believers' way of life. Catholic theology in particular has preserved this teaching. Personal prayer is recommended but is shown to be insufficient. In the circumstances of need, which are the human lot, and especially in those situations where Christian faithfulness is at stake, one must have recourse to the community:

"Are any among you suffering? They should pray. Are any cheerful? They should sing songs of praise. Are any among you sick? They should call for the elders of the church and have them pray over them, anointing them with oil in the name of the Lord. The prayer of faith

[22] In particular Deut 24:14-15; Lev 19:13; Isa 3:15; 5:7-10; Jer 5:26-30; Mal 3:5; Amos 2:6-8; 4:1; 8:4-8.

will save the sick, and the Lord will raise them up; and anyone who has committed sins will be forgiven. Therefore confess your sins to one another, and pray for one another, so that you may be healed. The prayer of the righteous is powerful and effective. . . .

"My brothers and sisters, if anyone among you wanders from the truth and is brought back by another, you should know that whoever brings back a sinner from wandering will save the sinner's soul from death and will cover a multitude of sins" (5:13-19).

The life of grace cannot be lived in isolation. Under its banal appearance, James is probably the New Testament document that shows this in the most concrete way.

3. First Peter is doctrinally richer than James' essentially pragmatic text. In it, tradition has found one of the most foundational presentations of the church as "holy priesthood" and "spiritual house" (1 Pet 2:5). But perhaps the reason for these designations has been insufficiently scrutinized.

From the beginning, the tone is sacramental. Indeed, the allusions to baptism seem clear (1:22, 23; see 3:21).[23] The letter is a *paraklesis*, that is, a writing of exhortation and consolation encouraging readers to keep their eyes trained on the goal. Now, the hope into which baptism plunges the believer is the opposite of a life selfishly turned in on itself:

"By the very fact of being united with Christ, believers are incorporated in his church. They no longer live for themselves but for the Lord and their neighbor. As a consequence, the new life which they claim is only an empty word if it is not expressed by 'mutual love,' in particular in the community."[24]

This is why, among the remnants of the old life that must be untiringly rejected, those which disparage mutual love and weaken com-

---

[23] See Marie-Émile Boismard, *Quatre hymnes baptismales dans la première épître de Pierre* (Paris: Cerf, 1961); John N. D. Kelly, *The Epistles of Peter and Jude*, Black's New Testament Commentaries 17 (1970; reprint, Peabody, Mass.: Hendrickson [1993?]) 15–20. In the introduction to the book of Jean-Claude Margot, *Les Épîtres de Pierre, commentaire* (Geneva: Labor et Fides, 1960) 11–13, Pierre Bonnard asks for a more nuanced interpretation since the only clear mention of baptism is in 3:21.

[24] Margot, *Épîtres de Pierre*, 31.

munal life (guile, hypocrisy, envy, slander [2:1]) are the most harmful (1:22-23). The ideal of a life founded on Christ is, on the contrary, a comportment marked by compassion, love of sisters and brothers, mercy, humility, refusal to render evil for evil or insult for insult, blessing (3:8-9), mutual submission, unity of spirit. And since what matters above all is the constant love for one another (4:8; see 1:22; 3:8), the author reminds readers of the duty of hospitality (4:9) and mutual service (4:10). The baptismal seed (1:23) is that of a gospel of love lived without hypocrisy. The list of these prescriptions, all of them based on love between sisters and brothers, is impressive. It will be enlightening to enumerate the most striking ones, one after the other:

"Now that you have purified your souls by your obedience to the truth so that you have genuine mutual love, love one another deeply from the heart. You have been born anew, not of perishable but of imperishable seed, through the living and enduring word of God" (1:22-23).

"Rid yourselves, therefore, of all malice, and all guile, insincerity, envy, and all slander" (2:1).

"Finally, all of you, have unity of spirit, sympathy, love for one another, a tender heart, and a humble mind. Do not repay evil for evil or abuse for abuse; but, on the contrary, repay with a blessing. It is for this you were called—that you might inherit a blessing" (3:8-9).

"Above all, maintain constant love for one another, for love covers a multitude of sins. Be hospitable to one another without complaining. Like good stewards of the manifold grace of God, serve one another with whatever gift each of you has received. Whoever speaks must do so as one speaking the very words of God; whoever serves must do so with the strength that God supplies, so that God may be glorified in all things through Jesus Christ. To him belong the glory and the power for ever and ever. Amen" (4:8-11).

"But let none of you suffer as a murderer, a thief, a criminal, or even as a mischief maker. Yet if any of you suffers as a Christian, do not consider it a disgrace but glorify God because you bear this name" (4:15-16).

"Now as an elder myself and a witness of the sufferings of Christ, as well as one who shares in the glory to be revealed, I exhort the elders among you to tend the flock of God that is in your charge, exercising the oversight, not under compulsion but willingly, as God would have you do it—not for sordid gain but eagerly. Do not lord it over those in your charge, but be examples to the flock. And when the chief shepherd appears, you will win the crown of glory that never fades away" (5:1-4).

Baptismal life, thus translated into relationships of mutual love and service, is in fact the life of "the holy priestly community," of the "spiritual house" where spiritual sacrifices pleasing to God through Jesus Christ are offered:

"It is by coming to him, a living stone rejected by human beings but chosen by God and precious in God's eyes, that you also, as living stones, are built into a spiritual house, in order to become a holy priestly community worthy of offering through Jesus Christ spiritual sacrifices pleasing to God.

"But you, you are the chosen race, the priestly community of the king, the holy nation, the people won by God so that you may proclaim the mighty acts of the one who called you out of darkness into God's marvelous light, you who once were not God's people but now are God's people; you who once had not obtained mercy but now have obtained mercy" (2:9-10).[25]

This passage is without doubt one of the most important of the New Testament. It boldly sees in the Christian community the people God was preparing, the "priestly community of the king" which, as a community, offers "spiritual sacrifices" through the holiness of its life. We shall come back to this.

The communion of believers in its totality is here qualified as priestly.[26] And it is in it, "the dwelling of the king," that the people of God offer spiritual sacrifices (*pneumatikai thusiai*). The context indicates

---

[25] [Author's translation. Throughout this book, the author uses several phrases from 1 Pet 2:5, 9 which are his translation of the Greek: "priestly community," "holy priestly community," "priestly community of the king," "priestly house," "priestly dwelling," "dwelling of the king," "priestly dwelling of the king." Ed.]

[26] We have studied this passage in "La Qualité sacerdotale du ministère," *NRT* 95 (1973) 481–514, and in "Sacerdoce," *DSp*, vol. 91 (1988) 7–10. The most satisfactory overall study is that of John Hall Elliott, *The Elect and the Holy: An Exegetical Examination of 1 Peter 2:4-10 and the Phrase* βασίλειον ἱεράτευμα (Leiden: Brill, 1966).

that these sacrifices are not primarily liturgical cultic actions but the existential acts of the holy life of this community. Its communion comes fundamentally from the Spirit, and it serves God in the daily actions of its members.[27] Through the "sanctification of the Spirit" (see 1:2), the sacrifice of Christ (see 1:19; 2:21-25) bears the community's fruits of the New Covenant.

Hence, it is from the people *as such* that the sacrifice which pleases and glorifies God, the sacrifice of holiness,[28] ascends to God. The whole letter is permeated by the conviction that this holiness—the form taken by life led in the "priestly community"—finds its material first of all in a specific relationship with others, even non-Christians.[29] This specific relationship is described in the prescriptions which we have singled out above. Thus the "mighty acts" of the One who has called God's people out of darkness into God's "marvelous light" (2:9) are proclaimed. Thus the Gentiles are enlightened by "honorable deeds" and will "glorify God when he comes to judge" (2:12). Thus husbands are won over to the word by their wives' conduct (3:1-2). Thus calumniators are confounded by the gentleness and reverence with which Christians give an accounting of the hope they have in their hearts (3:13-16). Thus the "presbyters" become examples to the flock by their behavior (5:3). To become holy "in all [one's] conduct" (1:15) means to place oneself, with faith and courage, within the network of relationships based on baptism which together make of the community, not a collection of persons seeking their own sanctification, but the unique and indivisible "royal priesthood," the "priestly community of the king," the "spiritual house" of God. In the holiness of all those whom the gospel has engendered "anew" (1:23; see 2:2), individual and community cannot be separated; however, the former is not sacrificed to the latter since the author of the letter never forgets the calling everyone has to enter "into an inheritance that is imperishable" (1:3-5; see 1:7). But the individual is a living stone of the "spiritual house" (2:5) only by remaining bonded to others and acting with the awareness of this bond, powered by the grace which incorporates

---

[27] See our article "Sacerdoce," 7–8. We have scrutinized this particular point at full length. We shall come back to it in chapter 3.

[28] See Elliott, *Elect*, 174–98: *"in 'spiritual sacrifices' no other idea is implied but the living of a holy life and the persistence in well-doing through the power of the Holy Spirit to the glorification of God."*

[29] Ibid., 185.

him or her into the "holy nation," the "priestly community." The church—for it is the church which is meant here—has for its flesh the network of mutual relationships created between the baptized by the "spirit of glory which is the Spirit of God" (4:14). The "holiness" of the faithful is woven into the fabric of the union of brothers and sisters, of "community" acting in communion.

IV. NEVER ALONE IN SALVATION

1. At the end of this rapid synthesis of the thinking of the New Testament writers on the "flesh of the church," one evident conclusion is inescapable. Without stretching or twisting the revealed texts, we have come to see the Christian way of life as radically determined by the presence at its core of what we have called the gospel relationship to others. What we are speaking of is the relationship of love between brothers and sisters *(agapē)* understood, not just as a feeling, an attitude of sympathy and affection toward the other, but also as the motivation for actions as concrete as the sharing of goods, hospitality, service, mutual forgiveness.

For the New Testament, this relationship with the other is not the object of an ethical demand superimposed on the essence of the Christian way of life and belonging to the category of supererogatory and meritorious acts. It is part of the essence of the Christian way of life; it is part of its very definition. One cannot be "in Christ" without being part of his body, therefore essentially joined to the other members of the body. One cannot be in the vine of God without being united to the other branches. One cannot be in the "priestly community," without being a "living stone" of the "spiritual house." The author of James would say that one cannot be in the faith without being in the charity that translates into works. The church exists by being *agapē;* the individual Christians exist by entering with their hearts and all their strength into this *agapē.* The church is the communion of men, women, and communities that the Spirit of God causes to live in solidarity through the force of the *agapē* that flowed with the water and the blood from the side of the One who "gave his life for his friends." Outside *agapē*—always implying reference to the other and others— there is only a corpse, a heap of dried-up branches, a mound of stones, an illusion.

2. The brief reports in Acts on the life of the first ecclesial community are, no one doubts it, more the expression of the ideal one would

have wished for than the description of an ideal actually realized.[30] Besides, the fraud of Ananias and Sapphira, the complaints of the Hellenists, accusing the Hebrews of neglecting their widows, show that not everything was perfect. However idealized, this description proves most significantly that from its origins the church was aware of its nature. The believers whom the risen Lord gathers in the fire of the Spirit are *before God* one heart and one soul in faith and prayer, in the sharing of spiritual and material goods, in the mutual relationships which the reign of God demands. Their living solidarity *(koinōnia)* is the realization of *agapē* under an extremely concrete form in which the relationship with God (which is the primary and determining factor) is never separated from the relationship with others.

It is in this sense that the church is *from God*. It is the communion of the faithful with God and among themselves, cemented by the *agapē* of hearts, hands, actions. This communion incarnates in humanity the quality of life—springing forth from the Father—which flows in Christ and in all those who together with him are one body, one vine, one "priestly community," one faith in action, in the Spirit. In this communion, the whole life of an individual is impelled forward, led to go beyond itself, to do away with its isolation. One member, one branch, one stone of the "priestly house" cannot exist simply for itself.

3. In this overall perspective, some passages of the New Testament assume a particular significance. Tradition noticed this and built on them its theology of the church. This is especially the case of three chapters in 1 Corinthians, chapters 10, 11, and 12. They deal insepara- bly with the Eucharist and the church. Without these chapters, we would know very little, not only of the Eucharist of the Lord, but also of the very nature of the church united to its Lord and unified within itself by a communion *(koinōnia)* whose source is wholly sacramental before being juridical.

Too many commentators deal separately with chapters 10, 11, and 12 of 1 Corinthians, which all speak of the body of Christ. It is clear that there is a link between the cup of 10:16-21 ("the cup of blessing") and that of 11:25-28 ("this cup is the new covenant in my blood. . . . Examine yourselves, and only then . . . drink of the cup"). Likewise,

---

[30] See *Church of Churches,* where we have commented on these texts and supplied a large bibliography. There are also bibliographical references on the notion of *koinōnia.*

there is a link between the broken bread of 10:16-17 ("the bread that we break") and that of 11:23-28 ("[he] took a loaf of bread . . . broke it . . . 'as often as you eat this bread'"), between "we who are many are one body" of 10:17 and "you are the body of Christ and individually members of it" of 12:27. The Corinthians may no longer partake of the sacrifice offered to demons because they are the body of Christ (10:17). But they are so because of "the bread that we break . . . is a sharing [koinōnia] in the body of Christ (10:16) of which the Lord says, 'this is my body that is for you'" (11:24). The broken bread and the shared cup effect the passage of the personal body of Christ to the body which believers are. And the ecclesial body is precisely the body in which the Spirit joins the diversity of the members in unity (12:13-14), incorporating them into Christ. The accent is placed on the relationship with Christ, source of the communion between sisters and brothers.

In chapter 11, Paul speaks again of the bond between the personal body of the Lord and the communion of brothers and sisters in one single body (which 10:16-17 was about). The communion between brothers and sisters is broken by schismata (divisions) (11:18), haireseis (factions) (11:19). These divisions and factions become concretely visible when all are gathered in one place (11:20) and as an assembly (11:18) manifesting the "church of God" (11:22) which is in Corinth— the very church Paul has greeted in the beginning of his letter—for the meal of the risen Lord. And at the table of the Lord (10:21), eating the bread of the Lord and drinking the cup of the Lord (11:27), which are, according to the word of the Lord himself (11:23), body of the Lord and blood of the Lord (11:27), they announce the death of the Lord (11:26) until he comes. Now, the Christians of Corinth transform this meal of the community as such, assembled by its Lord, into a collection of private, particular meals, each one eating her or his "own supper." They take the body of the Lord while contradicting its goal, willed by the Lord, which is that all those who share the one bread may be "one body" (10:17).

This is a very dense text. Paul condemns the Corinthians, reproves them by alluding to the example of the Israelites in the wilderness, whose trials "were written down to instruct us, on whom the ends of the ages have come" (10:11), trials he has just mentioned, and by alluding also to the case of those who offer sacrifices to idols (10:20-22). In the disease and death which will prevent people from being present at the time of the expected parousia (see 1 Thess 4:13-18), Paul sees a mark of God's censure of this conduct. For it is an insult to the death of the Lord proclaimed by the eating of the bread and the sharing of the cup (11:26), a counter-testimony to its vivifying power which is a power of communion (12:13; see Eph 2:13-17). To celebrate the meal of the Lord when one is cut off from one's brothers and sisters is tantamount to contradicting in action the very nature of the rite established by the Lord in order that the bread broken and distributed may create a community united in the communion of a single body.

Therefore, one cannot approach the table of the Lord "without discerning the body" (11:29). This expression has been the occasion of much commentary.[31] Everything leads one to side with those who refuse to separate the body of the Lord (because of the words "this is my body that is for you") and the ecclesial body (10:17; 12:13, 27). The bread of the table of the Lord speaks inseparably of both the Lord's personal body and the ecclesial body made up of the baptized. "Paul thinks inclusively more than exclusively."[32] Besides, he stresses that this lack of "discernment of the body" is connected with the way we "discern ourselves" (11:31 [author's translation]; see Rom 1:18; 14:13),[33] especially in regard to our imprisonment in egotism. The communion of the bread "recognized" (discerned) as body of the Lord is inseparable from the degree of communion with sisters and brothers existing in our own hearts. All have their own houses for eating and drinking at their own meals (11:22, 34). One comes to the assembly of the church of God in order to eat the meal of the Lord in communion with one's sisters and brothers, not to find a juxtaposition of individual meals.

This fusion of the theme of the Eucharist and the theme of the church, which Paul emphasizes, will become a determining factor for the great tradition. Whereas chapter 6 of John's Gospel will be the biblical locus in which the overtones of the inner grace of the Eucharist are suggested, 1 Corinthians—often paired with the lofty vision of the

[31] In order to document the diversity of opinions, see Barrett, *Second Corinthians,* 273–75; Geoffrey W. H. Lampe, "Church Discipline and the Interpretation of the Epistles to the Corinthians," in *Christian History and Interpretation: Studies Presented to John Knox,* ed. William R. Farmer and others (Cambridge, England: Cambridge University, 1967) 337–61 (346); Charles F. D. Moule, "The Judgment Theme in the Sacraments," in *The Background of the New Testament and Its Eschatology: In Honour of Charles Harold Dodd,* ed. William D. Davies and David Daube (Cambridge, England: Cambridge University, 1964) 464–91 (472–76); Albert Schweitzer, *La Mystique de l'apôtre Paul* (Paris, 1962) 225–40; [Albert Schweitzer, *The Mysticism of Paul the Apostle,* trans. William Montgomery (Baltimore: Johns Hopkins University, 1998)].

[32] Moule, "Judgment Theme," 473–74. See also Lampe, "Church Discipline," 473.

[33] This is well underlined by Moule, "Judgment Theme," 473.

author of Ephesians, which sees the body of Christ as a body of reconciliation—will be the biblical locus in which one will learn that "the Eucharist makes the church" in its mystical depth as body of the new humanity. The Eucharist is explained by the church, the church is explained by the Eucharist.

We are here at the very source of what is called the ecclesiology of communion. Although its ecumenical impact is due especially to the light it projects on the union of all the local churches in which the Eucharist of the Lord is celebrated in truth, its ecclesiological importance is due to its understanding of Christian life (communal and personal) as the consequence of the hold that the sacramental body of the Lord has on a believer's whole being. At the completion of Christian initiation, whoever has "eaten the [sacramental] body" of Christ Jesus, where the reconciliation of humankind takes place, can no longer live a solitary life. Whoever has drunk from the cup of the Lord can no longer live for herself or himself. As a member of the body, as a branch of the vine, as a living stone of the "priestly dwelling," one does not exist except for God and in communion with brothers and sisters. The moment of the greatest intimacy with the Lord—since one becomes his body—is also that of the greatest solidarity with others.

Ignatius of Antioch, whose works were for a long time in the same class as the apostolic letters, faithfully transmits the spirit of the gospel when he writes to the Magnesians:

"As the Lord, being united to the Father, did nothing without the Father, neither by himself nor through the apostles, so you are to do nothing without the bishop and presbyters. Do not try to make anything seem reasonable and proper for yourselves alone; but having come together in the same place, let there be one prayer, one supplication, one mind, one hope, in pure love and joy. There is one Jesus Christ, who is unexcelled. And so run together to the one temple of God, the one altar, the one Jesus Christ, who came forth from one Father and is with and has returned to the Father. . . .

"Those who were brought up in the old order of things now possess a new hope, no longer observing the Sabbath but living in the observance of the Lord's Day, on which our life has sprung up again through him and through his death."[34]

[34] Ignatius of Antioch, *Epistle to the Magnesians* 7.1-2, 9, in Roberts, 1:62. Compare Leo the Great, *Homily for the Anniversary of His Episcopal Ordination* 4.1, PL 54:148–49.

And with his customary eloquence, John Chrysostom will say:

"Nothing is more frigid than a Christian who cares nothing for the salvation of others. You cannot plead your poverty here, for she who gave her two copper coins shall be your accuser [Luke 21:1]. And Peter said, 'I have no silver or gold' [Acts 3:6]. And Paul was so poor that he was often hungry, and lacked necessary food [2 Cor 11:27; Phil 4:12]. . . .

"Do you not see the trees that bear no fruit, how strong they are, how beautiful, how large and smooth, how tall? But if we had a garden, we would much rather have pomegranates or fruitful olive trees. The others are for delighting the eyes, not for profit, which is small in them. Such are those who consider only their own interest. No, not even that much since these people are fit only for burning, whereas those trees are good for both building and the safety of those within. And such were those bridesmaids, chaste and decent and modest, but profitable to none [Matt 25:1-13]. . . . Such are those who have not nourished Christ. Notice that none of these are charged with particular sins of their own, with fornication, for instance, or with perjury, in short, with no sin except being of no use to another. Such was the one who buried the talent, showing indeed a blameless life but not being useful to another [Matt 25:25]. How can such a one be a Christian? Tell me, if the leaven, once it is mixed with the flour, does not change the whole into its own nature, would such a thing be leaven? And if a perfume emitted no sweet odor for those near it, could we call it a perfume? Do not say, 'It is impossible for me to persuade others [to become Christians]'—because if you are a Christian, it is impossible for it not to be so. Just as the natural properties of things cannot be denied, so is it here: *it is part of the very nature of a Christian*."[35]

The great tradition has not forgotten the conviction of the first Christian generations.[36]

For this reason, the solemn scene of the Judgment in Matthew (25:31-46) has always held a prominent place in the Christian conscience. This

[35] John Chrysostom, *Homilies on the Acts of the Apostles* 20.4, in Schaff, 11:133–34.

[36] Particularly under Anselm's influence, the Middle Ages will graft onto this conviction the *problem* of the mutual help of Christians in "satisfaction" and redemption, because the souls of the dead themselves could benefit by the prayers and "indulgences" of the living. See John Bossy, *Christianity and the West, (1400–1700)* (New York: Oxford University, 1985) 57–72.

gospel passage has given birth to thousands of religious foundations and undertakings of service. Whether "the least" mentioned in verses 40 and 45 are all unfortunate people or simply needy disciples, the evangelist's intention is clear. He wants to herald a mysterious identity between the Lord who judges from his throne as Son of Man (25:31, 32) and the immense throng of the "least." The reign is destined for all those who have always served the Lord (25:34). But they served above all when they touched him, loved him, helped him in the hungry (see Acts 6:1, 3; Rom 12:20; 1 Cor 11:33), the stranger (see Rom 12:13; Col 4:10; 1 Pet 4:9; Heb 13:2), the needy (see Acts 9:36-39; Jas 2:15-16), the sick (see 2 Tim 1:16, 18; Heb 13:3; Jas 5:14); the prisoner, the other. The sentence of the Last Judgment is the revelation in glory of what must constitute the fabric of the life of the church. The church cannot claim to serve the Father without serving the Lord in his relationship with "the least" of humans, the despised, the marginalized, the abandoned, in whose cries, tears, and wounds his cries, tears, and wounds are present. Between God and the elect there are always "the others."

Perhaps another word reported by Matthew suggests the same thing: "Where two or three are gathered in my name, I am there among them" (Matt 18:20), and then what they ask "will be done for [them] by my Father in heaven" (Matt 18:19).

This solidarity of communion comes from the bond between Christ and the Spirit into which Christians enter by baptism. Irenaeus perceived this when the church was beginning to reflect on its nature.

"This Spirit . . . [has] the power to admit all nations to life and open the New Covenant for them. [On Pentecost], *the Spirit brought distant tribes to unity and offered to the Father the firstfruits of all the nations.* This is why [the disciples], with one accord and in all languages, uttered praise to God [Acts 2:1-12]. And this is why the Lord promised to send the Advocate [John 16:7], who would join us to God. For just as dry flour cannot become a firm batch of dough or a loaf without liquid, *neither could we, being many, become one in Christ Jesus without the water from heaven.* And just as dry earth brings forth nothing unless it receives moisture, so we, being originally a dry tree, could never have brought forth fruit unto life *without the* gratuitous *rain* from above. For our bodies have received unity which leads to incorruption through the water of baptism; but our souls, through the Spirit."[37]

[37] Irenaeus, *Against Heresies* 3.17.1-3, in Roberts, 1:444–45.

* * *

The first letter of John will go back to the source of the breadth and depth of this communion:

"If we walk in the light as he himself is in the light, we have fellowship *[koinōnia]* with one another (1 John 1:7). We declare to you what we have seen and heard so that you also may have fellowship *[koinōnia]* with us; and truly our fellowship *[koinōnia]* is with the Father and with his Son Jesus Christ" (1 John 1:3).

Chapter 2

All Joined into One Body,
Eucharistic Body, Ecclesial Body

We just ended our survey of the New Testament data with texts
from Paul in which tradition has looked for the deepest secret of the
nature of the church. The fundamental intuition of Paul is that of a
mysterious correspondence between the body given at the eucharistic
table and the ecclesial body of the Lord. This agrees with what we
have discovered to be the common faith of the first apostolic communities: one is saved only by being "in Christ and his Spirit"; one is "in
Christ" only by being a member of the body, a branch of the vine, a
living stone of the "priestly house," a believer active in the charity of
"works"; one is all this in solidarity with others.

Such is the church of God, at least in the consciousness of the early
communities. They know that the church is built on the apostolic witness (dominated by the figure of Peter); it is woven with the bonds of
agapē with God and others, bonds created by the Spirit. Very rapidly, it
becomes unanimously accepted that this communion, into which the
Spirit introduces Christians at their baptism, is perfected at the table
of the Lord.

This ecclesiology of communion, sacramental and mystical before
becoming juridical and sociological, is the ecclesiology of what is called
the undivided church, the church of the centuries in which Constantinople—from which the communities that rejected the Council of
Chalcedon later on cut themselves off—and Rome are not yet separated.
The best way to verify this is to reread three contemporary Fathers of
the Church, from three different traditions, whose thought dominated
ecclesial life in the fifth century: Augustine for the West, John Chrysostom for Antioch, Cyril for Alexandria. A more extensive inquiry into
the works of the great representatives of patristic traditions would

demand a much longer work. But the conclusions of such a work would not say more than our restricted research.

I. A RITUAL OF MUTUAL LOVE

1. From the beginning, the bond between Eucharist and love for brothers and sisters is recognized by everybody. It is rooted in biblical soil. The Last Supper, celebrated around Jesus by the group of disciples, was a community meal. The ritual of the breaking of the bread at the beginning of the meal meant that a community was gathered around the table. The sharing of the cup symbolized the guests' consciousness of their deep communion in the same destiny.

The Jewish tenor of the Supper is obvious.[1] In order to show its roots in Jewish tradition, let us limit ourselves to quoting two texts by Flavius Josephus (d. ca. 100) evidencing that the paschal sacrifice took place in an atmosphere of loving accord:

"At the beginning of their feast called the Passover . . . they slay their sacrifices from the ninth hour until the eleventh, but in such a way that a group of at least ten are joined together for each sacrifice, for it is not lawful for them to feast alone."[2]

Without doubt, this was a "memory" of their origins. Because on the shores of the Red Sea,

"[Moses], having got the Hebrews ready for their departure and having sorted the people into tribes, kept them together in one place. But when the fourteenth day came and all were ready to depart, they offered the sacrifice and purified their houses with the blood, using bunches of hyssop for that purpose; and after they had eaten, they burnt the remainder of the flesh as if they were just about to depart. And to this day, we still offer this sacrifice in the same way."[3]

---

[1] We have often studied this. See our books and articles: *The Eucharist: Pasch of God's People*, trans. Dennis L. Wienk (Staten Island, N.Y.: Alba, 1967); "Eucharistie et Église," in Jean Zizioulas, Jean-Marie-Roger Tillard, Jean-Jacques Von Allmen, *L'Eucharistie*, Églises en dialogue 12 (Paris: Mame, 1970) 75–136; "La Sacramentalité de l'Église," in *Initiation à la pratique de la théologie*, ed. Bernard Lauret and François Refoulé, vol. 3 (Paris: Cerf, 1983) 385–466.

[2] Josephus, *The Wars of the Jews* 6.9, in Flavius Josephus, *The Works of Josephus*, trans. William Whiston (1736; reprint, Peabody, Mass.: Hendrickson, 1987) 749. [All quotations from this edition have been adapted by the editor.]

[3] Josephus, *The Antiquities of the Jews* 2.15, in ibid., 74.

Paul speaks of one bread broken, of one cup shared (1 Cor 10:17). But very early on, Christian tradition will strive to show that this one bread broken, this one cup given are themselves a multitude gathered in unity; therefore, the whole of the Eucharist is a mystery of communion, even in the elements used to celebrate it. It is communion creating communion.

2. The earliest known document here is a passage from the *Didache* (9.4), difficult to interpret but clear in its intuition. The prayer for the church rests on the sign of the bread, sacrament of the communion of all in the reign of God: "Just as this broken bread was scattered over the hills and became one when it had been brought together, so shall [your] church be brought together from the ends of the earth into [your] kingdom."[4] Whether what is meant in this text is the contrast between the sowing that throws the seed to the winds and the harvest that gathers the sheaves; or the making of bread from separate grains ground, kneaded, and baked together; or an allusion to the fragments remaining on "the hills" after the multiplication of the loaves, one point is certain: this ancient prayer proves that very early, the church has linked together Eucharist and unity.[5]

The image will pass into the great liturgies. It is found, within the account of the institution, in the *Euchologion* of Sarapion of Thmuis, friend of St. Athanasius (ca. 350). Here, however, the accent is not so much on the eschatological assembly as on the communion of the community threatened by heresy and schism:

"To you we offered this bread, the likeness of the body of the only-begotten. This bread is the likeness of the holy body. For the Lord Jesus Christ, in the night when [he] was handed over, took bread, broke it, and gave it to his disciples, saying: Take and eat, this is my body which is broken for you for the forgiveness of sins. Therefore, we also offered the bread making the likeness of the death. And we implore you through this sacrifice, God of truth: be reconciled to us all and be

[4] *Didache,* in *The Early Christians, in Their Own Words,* 4th ed., ed. Eberhard Arnold (Farmington, Penn.: Plough, 1997), 200–1.

[5] On this point, see Charles F. D. Moule, "A note on *Didachē* IX, 4," *Journal of Theological Studies* 6 (1955) 240–43; Lucien Cerfaux, "La Multiplication des pains dans la liturgie de la Didachè 9, 4–11," *Biblica* 40 (1959) 943–58; R. E. Goodenough, "John, a Primitive Gospel," *Journal of Biblical Literature* 64 (1945) 173–75. See Pseudo-Athanasius, *De Virginitate, PG* 28:265.

merciful. *And as this bread was scattered over the mountains and, when it was gathered together, became one, so also gather your holy church out of every nation and every region and every city and village and house, and make one living catholic church.* And we also offered the cup, the likeness of the blood. For the Lord Jesus Christ, taking a cup after supper, said to the disciples: Take, drink, this is the new covenant, which is my blood poured out for you for the forgiveness of sins. Therefore, we also offered the cup presenting the likeness of blood. God of truth, let your holy word come upon this bread in order that the bread may become body of the Word, and upon this cup in order that the cup may become blood of truth."[6]

About 380, the liturgy of the Apostolic Constitutions (7.25.3) does not modify the formula of the three prayers of the Eucharist which the compiler seems to have lifted from elsewhere. In contrast, the Anaphora of Der Balizeh, found in a sixth century papyrus, inserts it into the epiclesis and gives it its own character by adding the symbolism of the union of wine (recalling the vine of David) and the water (recalling the immolated Lamb):

"Fill us also with your glory, and deign to send your Holy Spirit on these offerings which you created, and make of this bread the body of our Lord and Savior Jesus Christ, and make of this cup the blood of the new covenant of our same Lord and Savior Jesus Christ. *And as this bread, formerly scattered over the heights, the hills, and the valleys, has been gathered to make a single body, and also as this wine, flowing from the holy vine of David, and this water, welling up from the immaculate Lamb, once mixed, have become one single mystery, in like manner, gather the catholic church of Jesus Christ.*

"For our Lord Jesus Christ, in the night when he was handed over, took bread in his holy hands, gave thanks, blessed it, sanctified it, broke it and gave it to his disciples and apostles. . . ."

3. It is probably in Africa about the middle of the third century that the symbolism of the wine and water appears explicitly. Cyprian adds it to that of the bread made of many grains and water. But he sees there, under one single sign, both the unity of Christians with Christ and their mutual unity:

[6] Serapion of Thmuis, *Euchologion*, in Maxwell Edwin Johnson, "The Prayers of Serapion of Thmuis" (Ph.D. diss., University of Notre Dame, 1992) 47.

"When the water is mixed with wine in the Chalice, *the people are united to Christ, and the multitude of the believers is bound and joined to him in whom they believe.* This association and mingling of water and wine are so mixed in the Chalice of the Lord that the mixture cannot mutually be separated. Whence *nothing can separate the church, that is the multitude* established faithfully and firmly *in the church*, persevering in what it has believed, *from Christ* as long as it clings and remains in undivided love.

"But thus, in the consecrating of the Chalice of the Lord, water alone cannot be offered, nor can wine alone. For, if anyone offers wine alone, the Blood of Christ begins to be without us. If, in truth, the water is alone, the people begin to be without Christ. But when both are mixed and, in the union, are joined to each other and mingled together, then the spiritual and heavenly Sacrament is completed. *Thus, in truth, the Chalice of the Lord is not water alone, or wine alone, unless both are mixed together just as flour alone or water alone cannot be the Body of the Lord unless both have been united and joined and made solid in the structure of one bread. By this Sacrament itself, our people are shown to be united; just as many grains collected in one and united and mixed form one bread, so in Christ, who is the heavenly Bread, we may know is one Body, to which our number is joined and united."* [7]

It is true that elsewhere, Cyprian uses in a simpler way the image of the cluster of grapes and the wine. It is in this simplicity—which the above reference to the water blurs—that the image will be received by the Western tradition:

"Finally, the very Sacrifices of the Lord declare that Christian unanimity is bound to itself with a firm and inseparable charity. For when the Lord calls Bread made from the union of many grains His Body, He indicates our people whom He bore united; *and when He calls Wine pressed from the clusters of grapes and many small berries and gathered in one His Blood, He, likewise, signifies our flock joined by the mixture of a united multitude."* [8]

---

[7] Cyprian, Letter 63.13, in Saint Cyprian, *Letters (1–81)*, trans. Rose Bernard Donna, CSJ, Fathers of the Church 51 (Washington: Catholic University, 1964) 211. This text is a reaction to the Aquarians.

[8] Cyprian, Letter 69.2, in ibid., 247–48.

4. Furthermore, the West strongly affirms that this unity is in no way a mere psychological union, an external unanimity, a concord based on purely human feelings. Hilary of Poitiers (d. 367) will say it in his *De Trinitate* (On the Trinity) that this unity is founded on God. Such is the fruit of baptism, which the Eucharist brings to fulfillment:

"The apostle Paul shows that this unity of the faithful arises from the nature of the sacraments when he writes to the Galatians, 'There is no longer Jew or Greek . . . all of you are one in Christ Jesus.' *Since these have one baptism and have all put on one Christ, is it from an agreement of will or from the unity of the sacrament that they are made one from so great a diversity of race and class, from both sexes? What will a concord of minds avail here when they are one because they have put on one Christ through the reality of one baptism? . . .*

"Now, how is it that we are in him through the sacrament of the flesh and the blood given us, as he himself testifies when he says: 'The world will no longer see me, but you will see me; because I live, you also will live. On that day you will know that I am in my Father, and you in me, and I in you' [John 14:19-20]. If he wanted to speak about a mere unity of will, why did he present a kind of gradation and sequence in the fulfillment of the unity, unless *he wanted us to believe that since he was in the Father through the nature of deity and we, on the contrary, in him through his birth in the flesh, he is in us through the mystery of the sacraments? Thus, a mediator teaches us perfect unity: we dwell in him, he dwells in the Father and, dwelling in the Father, dwells in us so that we might come to unity with the Father; for we live naturally in him who by birth lives naturally in the Father while he himself lives naturally in us as well.*

"He himself has testified how natural this unity is in us: 'Those who eat my flesh and drink my blood abide in me, and I in them' [John 6:56]. None will dwell in him except those in whom he himself dwells because the only flesh he has taken on is the flesh of those who have taken his. Now, he taught the mystery of this perfect unity, when he said, 'Just as the living Father sent me, and I live because of the Father, so whoever eats me will live because of me' [John 6:57]. Thus, he lives through the Father, and as He lives through the Father, we, in like manner, live through his flesh."[9]

The principal effect of the Eucharist—Scholastic theology will say *res eucharistiae*—is insertion into the body of Christ, a body whose

[9] Hilary of Poitiers, *On the Trinity* 8.8, 15–16, in Schaff and Wace, 9:139–40.

head is the risen Lord, a body made up of this head and its members, which are the baptized, a body vivified by the Spirit given by Christ who receives it from the Father. In the first centuries of Christianity, the West still had "initiation," which today is reserved for adults in the Latin rite whereas the East has preserved it as a law which admits of no exception: baptism, chrismation (anointing or confirmation), and Eucharist were inseparable. Within this ritual unit, the Eucharist was the sacramental moment symbolizing and sealing the incorporation of new members into the body from which they would draw their new life. We learn from Fulgentius, bishop of Ruspe (d. 533) that it is only after Augustine (d. 430) that the theological problem of the distinction between baptism and Eucharist was explicitly formulated.[10] Entrance into the church was climaxed by the eucharistic synaxis, into which baptism and anointing flowed.

II. AUGUSTINE, WITNESS OF THE WEST

1. When East and West were still united, Augustine was probably, among the Fathers of the church, the one who most explicitly and most profoundly expressed the link between the Eucharist (the summit of Christian initiation) and the church. Some of his statements have remained fundamental throughout the centuries. It seems useful to us to present at length the most typical of his texts, overlooked today by most Orthodox theologians and often forgotten by Western Protestants.

The best known document is probably Sermon 227, which is a homily given on Easter morning for those baptized during the paschal night:

"I haven't forgotten my promise. I had promised those of you who have just been baptized a sermon to explain the sacrament of the Lord's table, which you can see right now, and which you shared in last night. You ought to know what you have received, what you are about to receive, what you ought to receive every day. That bread which you can see on the altar, sanctified by the word of God, is the body of Christ. That cup, or rather what the cup contains, sanctified by the word of God, is the blood of Christ. It was by means of these things that the Lord Christ wished to present us with his body and

[10] Because, it seems, of the baptism of a child who died during the celebration before having received "the bread of life" (Fulgentius, Letter 12.24–26, in *PL* 65:390–92). See Aug. *Œuvres*, 37:810. In the West the discussions on the necessity of the Eucharist for salvation will be the result of this separation between baptism and Eucharist.

blood, which he shed for our sake for the forgiveness of sins. *If you receive them well, you are yourselves what you receive.* You see, the Apostle says, 'We who are many are one body, for we all partake of the same bread' (1 Cor 10:17). That's how he explained the sacrament of the Lord's table; one loaf, one body, is what we all are, many though we be.

"In this loaf of bread you are given clearly to understand how much you should love unity. I mean, was that loaf made from one grain? Weren't there many grains of wheat? But before they came into the loaf they were all separate; they were joined together by means of water after a certain amount of pounding and crushing. Unless wheat is ground, after all, and moistened with water, it can't possibly get into this shape which is called bread. In the same way you too were being ground and pounded, as it were, by the humiliation of fasting and the sacrament of exorcism. Then came baptism, and you were, in a manner of speaking, moistened with water in order to be shaped into bread. But it's not yet bread without fire to bake it. So what does fire represent? That's the chrism, the anointing. Oil, the fire-feeder, you see, is the sacrament of the Holy Spirit.

"Notice it, when the Acts of the Apostles are read. . . . *So the Holy Spirit comes, fire after water, and you are baked into the bread which is the body of Christ. And that's how unity is signified.*

"Now you have the sacraments in the order they occur. First, after the prayer, you are urged to lift up your hearts; *that's only for the members of Christ. After all if you have become members of Christ, where is your head? Members have a head.* If the head hadn't gone ahead before, the members would never follow. *Where has our head gone?* What did you give back in the creed? 'On the third day he rose again from the dead, he ascended into heaven, he is seated at the right hand of the Father.' *So our head is in heaven.* That's why, after the words 'Lift up your hearts,' you reply, 'We have lifted them up to the Lord.'

"And you mustn't attribute to your own powers, your own merits, your own efforts, this lifting up of your hearts to the Lord, because it is God's gift that you should have your heart up above. That's why the bishop, or the presbyter who's offering, goes on to say, 'Let us give thanks to the Lord our God,' because we have lifted up our hearts. Let us give thanks, because unless he had enabled us to lift them up, we would still have our hearts down here on earth. And you signify your agreement by saying, 'It is right and just' to give thanks to the one who caused us to lift up our hearts *to our head.*

"Then, after the consecration of the sacrifice of God, *because he wanted us to be ourselves his sacrifice, which is indicated by where that sacrifice was first put, that is, the sign of the thing that we are; why, thereafter the consecration is accomplished*, we say the Lord's prayer, which you have received and given back. After that comes the greeting, 'Peace be with you,' and Christians kiss one another with a holy kiss. *It's a sign of peace; what is indicated by the lips should happen in the conscience; that is, just as your lips approach the lips of your brothers or sisters, so your heart should not be withdrawn from theirs.*"[11]

The last paragraph of this long quotation is illuminated by book 10, chapter 6, of *The City of God*, which we will often comment upon and quote. But the most cogent text written by Augustine on this topic is probably Sermon 272:

"What you can see on the altar, you also saw last night; but what it was, what it meant, of what great reality it contained the *sacrament*, you had not yet heard. So what you can see, then, is bread and a cup; that's what even your eyes tell you; but as for what your faith asks to be instructed about, the bread is the body of Christ, the cup the blood of Christ. It took no time to say that indeed, and that, perhaps, may be enough for faith; but faith desires instruction. The prophet says, 'Unless you believe, you shall not understand' (Isa 7:9 [LXX]). I mean, you can now say to me, 'You've bidden us believe; now explain, so that we may understand.'

"Some such thought as this, after all, may cross somebody's mind: 'We know where our Lord Jesus Christ took flesh from; from the Virgin Mary. He was suckled as a baby, was reared, grew up, came to man's estate, suffered persecution from the Jews, was hung on the tree, was slain on the tree, was taken down from the tree, was buried; rose again on the third day, on the day he wished ascended into heaven. That's where he lifted his body up to; that's where he's going to come from to judge the living and the dead; that's where he is now, seated on the Father's right. How can bread be his body? And the cup, or what the cup contains, how can it be his blood?'

"The reason these things, brothers and sisters, are called *sacraments* is that in them one thing is seen, another is to be understood *[in eis aliud videtur, aliud intelligitur]*. What can be seen has a bodily appearance,

---

[11] Augustine, Sermon 227, in Hill, 6:254–55.

what is to be understood provides spiritual fruit. So if you want to understand the body of Christ, listen to the Apostle telling the faithful, 'Now you are the body of Christ and individually members of it' (1 Cor 12:27). *So if it's you that are the body of Christ and its members, it's the mystery meaning you that has been placed on the Lord's table; what you receive is the mystery that means you. It is to what you are that you reply Amen and by so replying you express your assent.* What you hear, you see, is the body of Christ, and you answer, Amen. *So be a member of the body of Christ, in order to make that Amen true.*

"So why in bread? Let's not bring anything of our own to bear here, let's go on listening to the Apostle himself, who said, when speaking of this sacrament, 'We who are many are one body' (1 Cor 10:17). Understand and rejoice. Unity, truth, piety, love. 'One bread'; what is this one bread? The one body which we, being many, are. Remember that bread is not made from one grain, but from many. When you were being exorcised, it's as though you were mixed into dough. When you received the fire of the Holy Spirit, it's as though you were baked. Be what you can see, and receive what you are *[estote quod videtis et accipite quod estis].*

"That's what the Apostle said about the bread. He has already shown clearly enough what we should understand about the cup, even if it wasn't said. After all, just as many grains are mixed into one loaf in order to produce the visible appearance of bread, as though what holy scripture says about the faithful were happening: 'Those who believed were of one heart and soul' (Acts 4:32); so too with the wine. Brothers and sisters, just remind yourselves what wine is made from; many grapes hang in the bunch, but the juice of the grapes is poured together in one vessel. That too is how the Lord Christ signified us, how he wished us to belong to him, *how he consecrated the sacrament of our peace and unity on his table.* Any who receive the sacrament of unity, and do not hold the bond of peace, do not receive the sacrament for their benefit, but a testimony against themselves."[12]

Similar expressions are found throughout Augustine's baptismal sermons that have come down to us. Thus:

"This bread is the body of Christ of which the Apostle speaks when he addresses the church: you are the body of Christ and its members" [see 1 Cor 12:27].[13]

[12] Augustine, Sermon 272, in ibid., 7:300–1.
[13] Augustine, Sermon Guelferbytanus 7, in *PL-S* 2:554–56; Aug. *Misc.*, 1:462–64.

Sometimes the language is even more strongly realistic:

"You are on the table and you are in the chalice, you along with us are this. We are this together. We are drinking this together because we are living it together. . . .

"Since what is realized is one reality, you too must be one by loving one another, by keeping one faith, one hope, one indivisible love. . . . *Nam et nos corpus ipsius sumus et per misericordiam ipsius quod accipimus nos sumus* (for we too have become his body and through his mercy we are what we receive). . . .

"You did not exist and you were created, that is, placed on the threshing floor of the Lord where the wheat was trampled by the labor of oxen, that is, the messengers of the gospel; during the period of your catechumenate, you were reserved in the granary; after registering your names, you were milled by fasts and exorcisms; then you came to the water and were kneaded in order to become one dough; by the heat of the Spirit you were baked and have become the Lord's bread."[14]

Augustine's idea is summed up well in a lapidary Latin phrase from *Guelferbytanus* Sermon 7: *quod accipitis vos estis, gratia qua redempti estis* (you are what you receive through the grace that redeemed you).[15] And the text continues, "You assent to it when you say *Amen*: what you see is the sacrament of unity *(sacramentum est unitatis)*.

Augustine refuses to separate the sacramental body, which is the eucharistic table (body *in mysterio*, *mystical* body, in the primary sense of this locution whose meaning will evolve),[16] and the ecclesial body of Christ (head and members). The eucharistic bread is the body of Christ. Since Christians are members of the body of Christ through baptism, they are truly this bread. *They receive what they are.* This is a bold vision, hardly explicated in fact, but extremely profound. By carrying the body and blood of Christ *in mysterio*, the sacrament carries the *objective* grace of communion, that is, of unity. It is the gift, not of a Christ isolated from the church, but of the head joined to the body. And this body of Christ is *inseparably* made up of the personal body of

---

[14] Sermon Denis 6, whose authenticity is sometimes questioned, but whose spirit is certainly Augustinian, in *PL* 46:834–36; Aug. *Misc.*, 1:29–32.

[15] Aug. *Misc.*, 1:463.

[16] See the fine book of Henri de Lubac, *Corpus Mysticum: l'Eucharistie et l'Église au Moyen Age, Étude historique,* 2nd ed. (Paris: Aubier, 1949).

the risen Christ and the members, that is, Christians bonded by the Spirit into a living communion. What would a body without members be? what would a body without a head be? what would a body in which head and members would be separate and joined only by a mere moral or psychological bond be?

2. Making his intuition more explicit, Augustine reaches to the deepest core of the link which thus joins Eucharist and church. The very heart of ecclesial life is bound to the sacrament of the Lord's body. For in its reality, the eucharistic sacrifice is the sacrament of the sacrifice of the ecclesial body *as such,* that is, *inseparably,* of the sacrifice of Christ as head surrounding the sacrifice of its members and of the sacrifice of the members incorporated into that of their head, which was offered "once for all":

"A true sacrifice is every work we do to be united to God in a holy community, every work which has a relation to that supreme good and end where we can be truly blessed. That is why even the mercy we show to others is not a sacrifice if it is not shown *for God's sake.* For sacrifice, even though made or offered by a human being, is a divine thing, as those who called it *sacrifice* wanted to show. *Thus, those consecrated in the name of God and vowed to God are themselves a sacrifice in so far as they die to the world so that they may live to God.* For this is a part of that mercy which people manifest to themselves; as it is written, 'Have mercy on your soul by making yourself acceptable to God.'

"*Our body is also a sacrifice when we discipline it by temperance* if, as we should, we do it *for God's sake* so that we might not make our members instruments of unrighteousness for sin but instruments of righteousness *for God.* The Apostle exhorts us to make this sacrifice when he says, 'I appeal to you therefore, brothers and sisters, by the mercies of God, *to present your bodies as a living sacrifice, holy and acceptable to God, which is your spiritual worship'* [Rom 12:1]. Consequently, if the body, which the soul uses as a servant or instrument because it is inferior to the soul, is a sacrifice when it is used rightly *and in relation to God,* how much more does the soul itself become a sacrifice when it *offers itself* to God so that, inflamed by the fire of divine love, it may partake of God's beauty and become pleasing to God, losing the form of worldly desire and being remolded into the image of immortal beauty? And this, indeed, is what the Apostle adds when he says, 'Do not be conformed to this world, but be transformed by the renewing of your minds, so that you may discern what is the will of God—what is good and acceptable and perfect' [Rom 12:2].

"Therefore, since true sacrifices are works of mercy to ourselves and others done in relation to God and since works of mercy have no other object than the relief of distress or the conferring of happiness and since there is no happiness apart from that good of which it is said, 'But for me it is good to be near God' [Ps 73:28], *it follows that the whole redeemed city, that is, the assembly or community of the saints, is offered to God as our sacrifice through the great high priest who, in the form of a slave, offered himself for us in his passion in order to make us the body of this glorious head.* It was this form he offered, he is offered in it, because it is thanks to it that he is mediator, that he is priest, that he is sacrifice. *Accordingly, after the Apostle exhorted us to 'present [our] bodies as a living sacrifice, holy and acceptable to God,* which is [our] spiritual worship,' and not to be 'conformed to this world, but [to] be transformed by the renewing of [our] minds, so that [we] may discern what is the will of God—what is good and acceptable and perfect,' that is, *the true sacrifice of ourselves*—he says: 'For by the grace given to me, I say to everyone among you, not to think of yourself more highly than you ought to think, but to think with sober judgment, each according to the measure of faith that God has assigned. For as in one body we have many members, and not all the members have the same function, so we who are many are one body in Christ, and individually we are members one of another. We have gifts that differ according to the grace given to us' [Rom 12:3-6]. *This is the sacrifice of Christians: we, being many, are one body in Christ. And this is also the sacrifice which the church continually celebrates in the sacrament of the altar, known to the faithful, in which the church teaches that it itself is offered in the offering it makes to God."*[17]

It was necessary to quote this fundamental text in its entirety; it is often known only by its last sentence cut off from its context.[18] It sheds light on a declaration of Sermon 227 already met with:

---

[17] Augustine, *City of God* 10.6, in Schaff, 2:183–84.

[18] In this sentence, we translate *frequentare* by "celebrate" and not "reproduce" (Aug. *Œuvres*, 34:449) which is ambiguous. On the meaning of *frequentare*, see Albert Blaise, *Dictionnaire latin-français des auteurs chrétiens* (Turnhout: Brépols, 1954), who explicitly cites this passage.

"[God] wanted us to be ourselves his sacrifice, which is indicated by where that sacrifice was first put, that is the sign of the thing that we are."[19]

The sacrifice *of* the totality and the sacrifice *in* its totality, this is for Augustine the contents of the Eucharist.

This identity between body received and body "brought back to God," "offered to God," "for God" has as its consequence that whoever is not in the living communion of the ecclesial body receives the eucharistic bread and cup ritually and not "spiritually": "Those who are not in the body of Christ cannot be said to eat the body of Christ."[20] Only those who are in the communion of all the members of Christ receive the eucharistic gift. For Christ gives his body only to those who are in his body. This intuition of a *circumincessio* ("a true mutual inhabiting") between sacramental body and ecclesial body confers its own characteristic tenor on Augustine's ecclesiology.

This is especially true of the pneumatological character of the body of Christ, which the Spirit makes the living sacrifice that glorifies the Father:

"'The bread that I will give for the life of the world is my flesh' [John 6:51]. *Believers know that this is the body of Christ if they do not neglect to be the body of Christ. That they become the body of Christ if they want to live by the Spirit of Christ. No one lives by the Spirit of Christ except the body of Christ.* My brothers and sisters, understand what I say. You are human beings; you have a spirit and a body. What I call a spirit is what you call the soul, what makes you human beings, for you are made of a soul and a body. And so you have an invisible spirit and a visible

---

[19] Augustine, Sermon 227, in Hill, 6:255.

[20] Here is the complete text: "The apostle says, 'Because there is one bread, we who are many are one body, for we all partake of the one bread' [1 Cor 10:17]. So those who are in unity with Christ's body (that is, with the Christian community), the sacrament of which the faithful have been accustomed to receive at the altar, are truly said to eat the body and drink the blood of Christ. And consequently, heretics and schismatics, being separated from the unity of this body, are able to receive the same sacrament, but with no profit to themselves, on the contrary, with harm because later on they will be severely judged rather than delivered. For they are not in that bond of peace which is symbolized by this sacrament. . . . *Those who are not in the body of Christ cannot be said to eat the body of Christ*" (*City of God* 21.25, in Schaff, 2:472).

body. Tell me, which of the two makes the other live? Does your spirit live because of your body, or your body because of your spirit? . . . *Do you also want to live by the Spirit of Christ? Be in the body of Christ. For surely my body does not live by your spirit. My body lives by my spirit and your body by your spirit. The body of Christ can live only by the Spirit of Christ.*

"This is why the apostle Paul, when he explains what this bread is, says, '*Because there is one bread, we who are many are one body*' [1 Cor 10:17]. *O mystery of kindness! O sign of unity! O bond of charity! Those who want to live have a place to live, have the means to live. Let them draw near; let them believe; let them be embodied that they may live. Let them not shrink from being made one with other members; let them not be rotten members which deserve to be cut off . . . let them be fair, fit, and sound members; let them cleave to the body; let them live for God by God; let them labor now on earth so as to reign later in heaven. . . .*

"Those who eat such bread do not fight with one another; for we who are many are one bread, one body. And by this bread, God makes people of one mind to dwell in the one house."[21]

So the Eucharist belongs with the mystery of Pentecost: in it the Lord gives the Spirit in the dynamic movement itself in which the believers are assembled into his one body. Body of Christ and life of the Spirit are radically inseparable:

"'One body,' says the apostle Paul, 'one body and one spirit' (Eph 4:4). Consider our own bodies and their parts. The body consists of many parts, and one spirit quickens all the parts. . . . What our spirit, that is our soul, is to the parts or members of our body, that the Holy Spirit is to the members of Christ, to the body of Christ. That's why the apostle, after mentioning one body, in case we should take it as a dead body—'One body,' he says.

But I ask you, is the body alive?
It's alive.
What with?
With one spirit. 'And one spirit.'"[22]

---

[21] Augustine, *Homilies on the Gospel of John* 26.13-14, in Schaff, 7:172.
[22] Augustine, Sermon 268, in Hill, 7:278–79.

Now, those who are one bread are the body of Christ in the indivisible Spirit:

"'But all these things one and the same Spirit worketh, dividing to every one according as he will' [1 Cor 12:11]; dividing, therefore, but not Himself, those diversities [which] are spoken of as members in the body, because the ears have not the same function as the eyes, and, so, divided, because He Himself is one and the same. Thus, different duties are harmoniously allotted to the different members. However, when we are in good health, in spite of these members being different, they rejoice in a common and equal health, all together, not separately, not one with more, another with less. *The head of this body is Christ, the unity of this body is proved by our sacrifice,* which the Apostle refers to briefly when he says: 'For we being many are one bread, one body' [1 Cor 10:17]. Through our Head we are reconciled to God because in Him the divinity of the only-begotten Son shared in our mortality, that we might be made sharers in His immortality."[23]

This last text mentions the eschatological dimension of the Eucharist. The Eucharist does not announce a purely individual bliss, limited to the eternal encounter of the baptized with God. The definitive life *in patria* (in the homeland), to which Christians aspire, will be that of the whole body, in the *societas sanctorum* (company of the saints). Now, this hope itself is in the sacrament of the eucharistic table:

"He said, 'For my flesh is true food and my blood is true drink' [John 6:55]. Indeed, by eating and drinking, people seek to neither hunger nor thirst, but this is provided only by this food and drink, which makes those who eat and drink it immortal and incorruptible, that is, by this same community of saints where full and perfect peace and unity will reign. This is why, as God's friends understood before us, our Lord Jesus Christ has given us his body and blood in things which are made one from many parts. For one bread is formed from many grains, and one wine is pressed from many grapes."[24]

[23] Augustine, Letter 187.20, in Augustine, *Letters,* 5 vols., trans. Sr. Wilfrid Parsons, S.N.D., Fathers of the Church (New York: Fathers of the Church, 1951–1955) 4:236–37.

[24] Augustine, *Homilies on John* 26.17, in Schaff, 7:173.

On the nature of eternal peace, Augustine will perhaps be more explicit elsewhere: "Only this peace of the heavenly city can be truly called and esteemed the peace of rational creatures, consisting as it does of the perfectly ordered and harmonious enjoyment of God and of one another in God."[25] The life of the body of Christ, into which the baptized are plunged and which is destined to blossom into eternal life, is not that of a communion *with Christ alone,* although it comes from him and his Spirit. It is a life *in* the body, the life *of* the body, whose beneficial effect par excellence is and remains communion. This communion, which is expressed here below by concord, peace, sharing, will in eternal life blossom into a single fulfillment of the human vocation in the same worship rendered to God. Communion is already and will be eternally for every believer the life of an "incorporated member." Christians live and will live only by being body of Christ, grains in the one bread, clusters in the one wine. The Eucharist (1) celebrates this life *of the body* (the company of the saints) awaiting life eternal, *makes it present* sacramentally by *making present* the personal body and blood of Christ—the head gathering its body in the power of the Spirit; (2) strengthens it and nourishes it by placing it in a true contact with its source; and (3) announces its finality and its consummation. Therefore, in the Eucharist there are not two bodies, the personal body and the ecclesial body. There is a sacramental coincidence and union of the two into one, in which the former surrounds the latter and irrigates it with its own life through the gift of its Spirit and in which the latter lets itself be seized by the former in order to become, *in it,* a living sacrifice to the glory of the Father.

Such is Augustine's vision. It is possible that it was influenced by a text from *On the Mysteries* by Ambrose of Milan (d. 397). Speaking of the Eucharist, Ambrose wrote:

"Believers, understand why he speaks of food and drink. There is no doubt about this. *He tells us, as you have read, that it is in us he is in prison, and in the same way, it is in us he eats and drinks.*

"And so the church, seeing so great a grace, bids its sons and daughters, bids its neighbors come together to the sacraments, saying, 'Eat, my neighbors, drink and be inebriated, my sisters and brothers.' What we are to eat, what we are to drink, the Holy Spirit has made clear to us elsewhere by the prophet, who says, 'O taste and see that

[25] Augustine, *City of God* 19.17, in Schaff, 2:413.

49

the LORD is good; / happy are those who take refuge in him' [Ps 34:8]. *Christ is in this sacrament because it is the body of Christ; therefore, it is not bodily food, but spiritual.* The Apostle also says of its prefiguration that 'all ate the same spiritual food, and all drank the same spiritual drink' [1 Cor 10:3-4]. *For the body of God is a spiritual body; the body of Christ is the body of the divine Spirit because Christ is spirit,* as we read, *'The spirit before our face is Christ the Lord'* [see Lam 4:20 LXX]. And in the letter of Peter we have, 'Christ also [died] for us' [1 Pet 2:21]. Thus, this food 'strengthens' our 'heart,' and this drink 'gladdens the human heart' [Ps 104:15], as the prophet has declared."[26]

But it is evident that Augustine integrates this view (if he received it from Ambrose) into an immensely rich synthesis. The Spirit from which every baptized person lives is the Spirit of the entire body. This Spirit transcends the individual since it is the Spirit of Christ. It goes beyond the individual since it is in all. It is in the head in order to be in the body. What is more, since Pentecost, it is not in the head without being in the body. By rendering it present *in truth* in the bread and the cup, the Eucharist celebrates the personal body of the Lord Jesus Christ *in the act of giving life* to his ecclesial body through the Holy Spirit. It gives the personal body in the indissoluble bond that unites it to the ecclesial body.

It is precisely here that the mystery of the church lies. This is why the Eucharist celebrates and gives the church by celebrating and giving the body and blood of Christ:

"He wanted this food and drink to be understood as the community of his own body and members, which is the holy church in its saints and believers, predestined, called, justified, and glorified. Of these, the first has already taken place, namely, predestination; the second and third, that is, the call and justification, have taken place, are taking place, and will take place; but the fourth, glorification, now it exists in hope, later it will be a reality. *The sacrament of this reality, the unity of the body and blood of Christ, is prepared on the Lord's table,* in some places daily, in others at certain intervals of days; and *it is taken at the Lord's table,* by some to life, by some to death, but the reality itself, to which the sacra-

---

[26] Ambrose, *On the Mysteries* 57–58, in *Des Sacrements,* rev. ed., trans. and ed. Bernard Botte, SC 25 bis (1961), 127–28; [also in *On the Sacraments and On the Mysteries,* rev. ed., trans. T. Thompson, ed. J. H. Srawley (London: S.P.C.K., 1950) 150–51].

ment refers, is life for everyone and death for no one, no matter who takes part in it."[27]

The church is not the sum total of the baptized, but their "common life," that is, their communion in the indivisible Spirit of Christ, their life in communion, which reaches all the way into God. The Eucharist is the sacrament of this.

"The banquet of the Lord is the unity of the Body of Christ, not only in the sacrament of the altar, but also in the bond of peace."[28]

3. A contemporary of Augustine, Gaudentius of Brescia (d. 410), a friend of Ambrose and a follower of Chrysostom, had taken up the image of the bread made of many grains and the wine made of many grapes:

"As there are many grains of wheat in the flour of which bread is made by mixing it with water and baking it with fire, so also we know that many members make up the one body of Christ which is brought to maturity by the fire of the Holy Spirit. Christ was born of the Holy Spirit, and since it was fitting that he should fulfill all justice, he entered into the waters of baptism to sanctify them. When he left the Jordan he was filled with the Holy Spirit who had descended upon him in the form of a dove. As the evangelist tells us: 'Jesus, full of the Holy Spirit, returned from the Jordan' [Luke 4:10].

"Similarly, *the wine of Christ's blood, drawn from the many grapes of the vineyard that he had planted, is extracted in the winepress of the cross. When [people] receive it with believing hearts, like capacious wineskins, it ferments within them by its own power.*

"And so, now that you have escaped from the power of Egypt and of Pharaoh, who is the devil, join with us, all of you, in receiving this sacrifice of the saving passover with the eagerness of dedicated hearts. Then in our inmost being we shall be wholly sanctified by the very Lord Jesus Christ whom we believe to be present in his sacraments, and whose boundless power abides for ever."[29]

[27] Augustine, *Homilies on John*, 26.15, Schaff 2:173.

[28] Augustine, Letter 185.24, in Augustine, *Letters*, 4:166.

[29] Gaudentius of Brescia, *Paschal Homily 2*, in *The Liturgy of the Hours according to the Roman Rite*, vol. 2: *Lenten Season, Easter Season*, trans. International Commission on English in the Liturgy (New York: Catholic Book, 1976) Office of Readings, Thurs. of 2nd wk. of Easter, 2nd reading, p. 670.

Augustine's thinking is part of a tradition. It is not isolated; one century later, it is found again in Fulgentius, bishop of Ruspe, in North Africa:

"This spiritual upbuilding of the Body of Christ which happens in love (since according to the words of the blessed Peter '. . . like living stones, let yourselves be built into a spiritual house to be a holy priesthood, to offer spiritual sacrifices acceptable to God through Jesus Christ' [1 Pet 2:5]) this spiritual upbuilding, I say, is never more opportunely sought than *when the very Body and Blood of Christ are offered by the body of Christ itself (which is the church) in the sacrament of the bread and chalice:* 'The cup of blessing that we bless, is it not a participation in the blood of Christ? The bread that we break, is it not a participation in the body of Christ? Because the loaf of bread is one, we, though many, are one body, for we all partake of the one loaf' [1 Cor 10:16-17].

"And therefore, we ask that by that very grace by which it comes about that the church becomes the Body of Christ, by the same grace it may happen that all the members of charity, with the binding framework remaining, persevere in the unity of the Body. This we seek worthily to happen in us by the gift of that Spirit who is one Spirit of both the Father and the Son; because the Holy Trinity, by nature unity and equality and love, which is the one, only, and true God, *in total accord sanctifies those whom it adopts. . . .* [This is why it is said] '[T]he love of God has been poured out in our hearts through the Holy Spirit that has been given to us' [Rom 5:5]. . . .

"The love of God which has been poured out in our hearts through the Holy Spirit that has been given to us brings it about that they may return and become a spiritual sacrifice. . . . The church can always receive the grace of spiritual love through which it can continuously show itself a living and holy victim, pleasing to God."[30]

This living sacrifice is that of a life led in faith:

"'God's love has been poured into our hearts through the Holy Spirit that has been given to us.' For it is precisely the participation in the body and blood of the Lord, when we eat his bread and drink his

[30] Fulgentius, *To Monimus* 2.11.1-3, 12.4, in *Fulgentius: Selected Works,* trans. Robert B. Eno, Fathers of the Church 95 (Washington, D.C.: Catholic University, 1997) 250–51, 254.

blood, that urges us to die to the world by having our life hidden in God and to crucify our flesh with its passions and its lusts.

"Thus, all the faithful, who love God and their neighbors, although they do not drink from the cup of bodily passions, drink however from the cup of the Lord's love. Once inebriated by it, they must put to death what is still earthly; let those who have put on Jesus Christ no longer abandon themselves to the desires of the flesh, let them not look at what is visible but at what is invisible.

"To practice holy charity is to drink from the Lord's cup. Without charity, to give one's body to be burned would be useless [see 1 Cor 13:2]. The gift of charity effects this in us: that we may truly be what we celebrate in sacrament."[31]

We shall come back at length to this essential point. Here we shall limit ourselves to remarking that Augustine's theology became inscribed in the memory of the West. Because of it, the West conceived the essence of the church as being founded in mystery. This foundation is seen as the work of the pasch in the very act of bearing fruit in the flesh of human history. The church is the salvation which the Spirit actualizes by introducing believers into the body of reconciliation that was Christ's on the cross. The Eucharist has this effect in God's plan. It is the sacrament of the mystery.

Thomas Aquinas (d. 1274) shows that Western theological tradition continued to uphold this conviction for a long time. In the treatise on the Eucharist in the *Summa Theologica* he states that the *res* (the effect itself) of this sacrament "is the unity of the mystical body, without which there can be no salvation; for there is no entering into salvation outside the church, just as in the time of the deluge there was none outside the Ark, which denotes the church, according to 1 Pet 3:20-21."[32] Elsewhere, he adopts the viewpoint of John of Damascus: "This sacrament has a . . . significance . . . with regard to the present . . . that is, ecclesiastical unity, into which people are incorporated through this sacrament; that is why it is called *communion* or *synaxis*. For Damascene says, 'It is called *communion* because through it we communicate with Christ, both by partaking of his flesh and divinity and by communicating with and being united to one another through it' [*Exposition*

---

[31] Fulgentius, *Against Fabian* 28.16-19, in *Sancti Fulgentii episcopi Ruspensis Opera*, ed. J. Fraipont, CCL 91A (1968) 813–14.

[32] *ST IIIa*, q73, a3, pp. 236–37.

of the Orthodox Faith 4.13]."[33] Aquinas even makes it more precise: "Now, this sacrament has a twofold reality [*res*] . . . what is signified and contained, namely, Christ himself, and what is signified but not contained, namely, Christ's mystical body, which is the community of saints. Therefore, whoever receive this sacrament thereby express that they are made one with Christ and incorporated in his members."[34] The same ideas recur in Aquinas' commentary on John, with a telling explanation: "Those who eat and drink *spiritually* (and not in a purely external and merely ritual way) become partakers of the Holy Spirit, by whose action we are united to Christ and made members of the church."[35] For "with regard to the reality simply signified, those eat spiritually who are incorporated into the mystical body by a union of faith and charity. . . . This is effected by the Holy Spirit."[36]

III. THE CHURCH IS CATHOLIC BECAUSE IT IS A COMMUNION

1. Understood as a true mutual inhabiting of Christ (in his personal being as the risen One) and his ecclesial body—*circumincessio* whose sacrament is the Eucharist—the church becomes for Augustine the locus of the *agapē* of God. This *agapē* is accomplished in a communion between Christ as head and his members; this communion is so profound that at the limit, it admits only of one difference between him and them: only he is the eternal Son of the Father and only he saved them and continues to save them by his *agapē*. This salvation through *agapē* and communion is realized in this: in his historical work, the Son assumed *everything* in the human condition (by taking it on himself); at the same time, since the resurrection, he continues to live in his members the human tragedy in all its truth and all its reality. What this means is not "continued incarnation" but the fulfillment *(teleiōsis)* of the work of incarnation, in the power of the Spirit. Thus, the church is catholic. Indeed, catholicity does not mean simply material expansion into all parts of the world, but along with this expansion, actualization of the pasch in everything human.

---

[33] Ibid., q73, a4, p. 239.

[34] Ibid., q80, a4, p. 375. See what Cajetan writes in Tommaso de Vio Cajetan, *In de ente et essentia d. Thomas Aquinensis IIa-IIae,* 39.1, on the relationship between the *whole* and the members.

[35] Thus *On John* 6, *lect.* 6.3, in Thomas Aquinas, *Super Evangelium S. Ioannis lectura,* 5th ed., ed. Raphael Cai (Rome: Marietti, 1952), no. 972.

[36] Ibid., nos. 973, 976.

Augustine unceasingly comes back to this intuition which was to be of supreme importance for the christology and ecclesiology of the West.[37] The text which is most packed with meaning is probably that commentary on Psalm 101, which has been echoed in numerous other excerpts:

"Christ sings this. If it is only the head that sings, this song comes from the Lord and does not concern us. But if it is the whole Christ, that is, the head and the body, be among the members, cling to him through faith, hope, and charity. *And then, here you are, singing in him and exulting in him because he himself toils in you, thirsts in you, is hungry and in tribulation in you. He again dies in you and you, in him, are already risen. For if he did not die in you, he would not ask that the persecutor spare him in you by saying, 'Saul, Saul, why do you persecute me?'* [Acts 9:4]. Therefore, my brothers and sisters, it is Christ who sings, and you know how: this Christ, as we already have explained to you, and I know that these things are not unknown to you. *The Lord Christ is the Word of God, through whom all has been made. This Word became flesh and dwelt in our humanity in order to redeem us.* The God greater than all, the Son equal to the Father, became human. *He became human to be, as Human-God, the mediator between God and humankind, to reconcile those who were far, to reunite those who were separated, to recall those who had left, to bring back those who were lost: this is why he became human. He accordingly became head of the church; he has a body and members. Look for his members; right now they groan over all the earth;* later on, at the end, they will rejoice in 'the crown of righteousness,' which, Paul says, 'the Lord, the righteous judge, will give [us] on that day' [2 Tim 4:8]. And so, let us now sing in hope, *all joined together in unity.* Clad as we are with Christ, *we are all, together with our head, Christ.* . . . It is therefore obvious that we belong to Christ and *that being his members and his body, we are, with our head, one human being.* Consequently, let us sing, 'I will sing of loyalty and of justice; to you, O LORD, I will sing'" [Ps 101:1].[38]

---

[37] See the study of Pasquale Borgomeo, *L'Église de ce temps dans la prédication de saint Augustin* (Paris: Études augustiniennes, 1972) especially 209–34. M. J. Sheridan, *The Theology of the Local Church in Vatican II* (Rome, 1980) 6, 85, uses the term *circumincessio* in another context.

[38] *En in Ps* 100 [101].3, in *PL* 37:1284–1285 and *CCL* 39:1408; see *in Ps* 3, in *PL* 36:77; *in Ps* 37 [38], in *PL* 36:411; *in Ps* 39 [40], in *PL* 36:436; *in Ps* 40 [41], in *PL* 36:459; *in Ps* 58 [59], in *PL* 36:694; *in Ps* 86 [87], in *PL* 37:1107. See also, *in Ps* 101 [102], *Sermon* 1,

The result of the incarnation is "one human being" encompassing all the faithful (in communion) "in Christ" through *agapē*: the head and the members are a single Christ, "the head in heaven, the members below; for one suffering neither hardship nor pain would say, 'Saul, Saul, why do you persecute me?'" We are with him in heaven through hope, he is with us on earth through charity.[39]

So "the whole human being is he and we . . . the fullness of Christ is head and members . . . Christ and the church."[40] In this totality, Christ remains inseparable from his ecclesial body: "All the trials, temptations, and suffering his church undergoes in this world, it is he who suffers them."[41] Thus, Augustine ends by giving the suffering of Christians an authentic ecclesiological and eschatological dimension:

"How can there be in the body of a single human being this magnitude so immense that it may be slain by all? But we ought to understand that it is we, the church, the body of Christ. *For Jesus Christ is one human being with head and body, the savior of the body and of the members of the body: two in one flesh, in one voice, in one passion, and when iniquity shall have passed away, in one rest.*

"Hence, *the sufferings of Christ are not just in Christ, or better, are not only in Christ.* If you understand Christ to be head and body, the sufferings of Christ are in Christ alone; but if you understand Christ to be just the head, the sufferings of Christ are not only in Christ. . . . *Therefore, if you are listening to me, whoever you are, are among the members of Christ* (or rather—you hear me—if you are united with the members of Christ), *anything you suffer from those who are not among the members of Christ, was wanting in the sufferings of Christ* [see Col 1:24]. It is added because it was wanting; you fill up the measure, you do not make it run over. You suffer exactly as much as was to be contributed from your sufferings to the whole suffering of Christ, who suffered as our head and still suffers in his members, that is, in us. Into this common treasury, each of us pays what we owe according to our ability, and according to our strength, we contribute our share of sufferings. *The*

in *PL* 37:1295; *in Ps* 118 [119], in *PL* 37, 1594; *in Ps* 119 [120], in *PL* 37:1602; *in Ps* 140 [141], in *PL* 37:1819.

[39] *Exp on Ps* 53 [51].1, in Schaff, 8:202.

[40] Augustine, *Homilies on John* 21.8, in Schaff, 7:140. See also *Sermon* 133.8, in Hill, 4:338.

[41] *En in Ps* 62 [63].2, in *PL* 36:749 and *CCL* 39:794.

storehouse of all human beings' sufferings will not be filled until the end of the world."[42]

And elsewhere:

"Being in affliction, the body of Christ groans, and until the end of the world, when afflictions pass away, this human being groans and calls upon God; and each one of us, according to our measure, has a part in that cry of the whole body. You have cried in your time and your time has passed away; another has come after you and cried in her days. You here, that one there, another elsewhere: the body of Christ cries every day, members departing and succeeding one another. *One human being endures to the end of the world; it is the members of Christ who cry."*[43]

Augustine can conclude that "Christ still undergoes trials, not in his flesh in which he ascended to heaven, but in my flesh which still labors on earth."[44] In his body, throughout all nations, he shows himself to be "in great tribulation."[45] He also deduces that Christ prays in his body:

"He prays for us, as our priest; *he prays in us, as our head;* he is prayed to by us, as our God. *Let us therefore recognize our words in him and his words in us.* . . . We pray to him in the form of God, he prays in the form of a slave; there the creator, here the created, he puts on, himself unchanged, the creature so that it might be changed, and makes us with himself one human being, head and body. Therefore, we pray to him, through him, in him; and we pray with him, *he prays with us; we speak in him, he speaks in us the prayer of this psalm."*[46]

Christ speaks in his body:

"It is in Christ that the church speaks and in the church that Christ speaks, the body in the head and the head in the body."[47]

---

[42] *Exp on Ps* 62 [61].2, in Schaff 8:251–52.

[43] Ibid. 86 [58].5, in Schaff 8:411.

[44] *Exp on Ps* 143 [142].3, in Schaff, 8:649. See also Letter 55.7.31, in Augustine, *Letters*, 1:273–74.

[45] *Exp on Ps* 61 [60].2, in Schaff, 8:249.

[46] Ibid. 86 [85].1, in Schaff, 8:410.

[47] *En in Ps* 30 [31].2.4, in *PL* 36:232 and *CCL* 38:193.

Already before the incarnation, *jam ab Abel justo* (from the righteous Abel on), this communion was lived by the righteous among the people of God; they were also linked to the ecclesial body by their faith and obedience:

"All those things we read in holy Scripture were written before the Lord's coming for one reason, to press his coming upon our attention and to signal the future church, that is, *the people of God throughout all nations, the church which is his body, where all the saints are united and numbered, all the saints who have ever lived, even before his advent, and who believed then in his future coming, just as we believe in his past coming.* Here is an illustration: at the time of his birth but while still in the womb, Jacob put out a hand with which he held the foot of his brother, who was being born before him, then came Jacob's head and finally the rest of his members [Gen 25:26]. Nevertheless, the head surpasses in dignity and power, not only those members which followed it, but also the very hand which preceded it at birth; and it is really the first, not according to the time it appeared but according to the order of nature. Likewise, *the Lord Jesus,* the mediator between God and humanity [1 Tim 2:5], 'who is over all, God blessed forever' [Rom 9:5], before he appeared in the flesh and came forth in some way from the womb of his mystery as a human being to the eyes of human beings, lets us see *in the person of the holy patriarchs and prophets a certain part of his body, like a hand which he gave as a token of his own approaching birth* and with which he supplanted the proud people who came before him, using the bonds of the Law as if they were his five fingers. Through five epochs his own destined coming was foretold and prophesied without cease; moreover, he through whom the Law was given wrote the five books. The open hand of Christ did not fill with blessing the proud, who were carnally minded and sought to 'establish their own [righteousness]' [Rom 10:3], but the tightly closed hand banned them from such good; and therefore their feet were tied and 'they will collapse and fall, / but we shall rise and stand upright' [Psalm 20:8]. *But even though, as I have said, the Lord Christ sent a certain part of his body ahead of him in the saints who were born before him: nevertheless, he himself is the head of the body, the church [Col 1:18], and all these saints have been attached to this body, of which he is the head, in virtue of their believing in him whom they announced prophetically. For they were not separated from that body because they came before him; rather, they were made one with it because of their obedience. Indeed, the hand may appear before the head, yet it is united and subordinate to the head.* All the things which were written in the past were written so that they might teach us [see Rom 15:4]; they are figures for us and what happened to these people is a figure. Moreover, they were written for our sakes, 'on whom the ends of the ages have come'" [1 Cor 10:11].[48]

In the psalmist's cries and thanksgiving, Christ Jesus already suffers, prays, speaks in his body. This is why the church recognizes there its own heirloom.

2. The communion with Christ and his members, which was to be fully actualized at the resurrection, was already, as it were, the soul of his historical mission. For he was carrying in himself, mystically and through divine *agapē*, the authentic human condition. He lived it, in some way "recapitulating" it. He "received" it, he the Son of God, and this "receiving" put its mark on it:

"He transferred us into himself by a figure when he willed to be tempted by Satan. But just now we read in the gospel how the Lord Jesus Christ was tempted by the devil in the wilderness. The whole Christ was tempted by the devil. *In Christ you were tempted because Christ himself took flesh from you to give you salvation; he took death from you to give you life; he took revilings from you to give you honor; thus, he took temptation from you to give you victory.* If we have been tempted in him, in him we overcome the devil.

"Recognize that in him you are the one who is tempted and then recognize that in him you are the one who is victorious. He could have sent the devil away; but if he had not been tempted, he would not have taught you, who must undergo temptation, how to win victory over it."[49]

This brings to mind Irenaeus, who had already written in *Against Heresies:*

[48] Augustine, *Catechizing the Uninstructed* 3, in Schaff, 3:285–86. On "ab Abel," see *Sermon* 341.9, 11, in Hill, 10:24, 26. See Yves Congar, "Ecclesia ab Abel," in *Abhandlungen über Theologie und Kirche, Festschrift für Karl Adam,* ed. Marcel Reding (Düsseldorf: Patmos, 1952) 79–110. Compare the view of Augustine with that of Gregory of Nyssa, *On the Song of Songs,* Homily 3, PG 44:909.

[49] *Exp on Ps* 61 [60].3, in Schaff, 8:249. [The second paragraph of this quotation is the translator's work. Ed.]

"[The Spirit] descended upon the Son of God, made the Son of Man, *in order to accustom itself, in fellowship with him, to dwell in the human race, to rest with human beings, and to dwell in the handiwork of God, working the will of the Father in them,* and renewing them from their old habits into the newness of Christ."[50]

3. Therefore, head and body form a single communion. On this earth, its reality and depth find their seal in the sacraments. While Christ gave birth to the church on the cross (in water, blood, and Spirit), the church gives birth to "those who have been washed by the baptism of Christ and have become partakers of his body and blood,"[51] thereby giving birth to Christ since it gives him his members (in the power of the Spirit):

"You to whom I speak, you are the members of Christ. And who gave you birth? I hear the voice of your hearts: 'Our mother the church. . . .' That the church gives birth is proved by you yourselves because you were born from it. Now, since you are the members of Christ, the church gives birth to Christ. . . . Yes, we dare to call ourselves the mother of Christ. Having said that we are all his sisters and brothers, why should I not dare to say that we are his mother?"[52]

Sermon 213 connects this fecundity with the economy of the incarnation:

"The church is a virgin. You're going to say to me, perhaps, *'If she is a virgin, how does she give birth to children? Or if she doesn't bear children, how is it we gave in our names to be born of her womb?'* I answer: she is both virgin, and she gives birth. She imitates Mary, who gave birth to the Lord. Didn't the virgin, Saint Mary, both give birth and remain a virgin? *So too the church both gives birth and is a virgin. And if you really think about it, she gives birth to Christ, because those who are baptized are his members, parts of his body.* 'You,' says the apostle, 'are the body of Christ, and members of it'" (1 Cor 12:27).[53]

---

[50] Irenaeus, *Against Heresies* 3.17.1, in Roberts, 1:444.

[51] Augustine, *City of God* 21.25.2, in Schaff, 2:472.

[52] Augustine, *Sermon* Denis 25.8, in *PL* 46:938 and Aug *Misc*, 1:163.

[53] Augustine, *Sermon* 213.8, in Hill 6:145.

IV. BODY OF COMMUNION

1. Such is the church of God, connected to the "mystery" by its constitutive bond with the Eucharist, in which the initiation is perfected and then is reactualized throughout the whole life of the believer. Originating in the eternal communion of the Father, Son, and Spirit,[54] it is the communion which results from what Augustine perceives as the "passage" of the life of the risen Lord into all believers, and the "passage" (the pasch) of all believers into the one and indivisible life of the risen Lord. For Augustine does not separate the two movements, the one going from Christ to the faithful and the one going from the faithful to Christ; these are the two inseparable sides of the work of the Spirit. The reality of the communion is due to this twofold movement. For the faithful "pass" into Christ with their cries of pain and of "suffering for the faith," which become Christ's; their human roots and their solidarities, which become Christ's; their joys and their victories, which become Christ's; their hopes and their failures, which become Christ's. And Christ "passes" into the faithful with his cross, which becomes his members'; his victory and his resurrection, which become his members'; his work of reconciliation, which becomes his members'; his communion with the Father, which becomes his members'. The result is that the faithful are but one body *of* Christ and one body *in* Christ, in a concrete unity which is not of the sociological order—since it is due to their being seized by the Spirit of God—but which nevertheless assumes the density and variety of all that is human. Here is the church of God, in its innermost depth.

The ecclesial body of Christ is not an addition of members, a quantitative whole. For to be a member of this body does not mean first of all to add one unit to the number of others. It is, fundamentally, to let oneself be integrated by the Spirit of the Lord into the communion in which the totality of what is human—with its differences, its diversity, its joys, and its sorrows—has become one with Christ Jesus in the *agapē* of the cross and resurrection. The body of Christ is a body of communion. At the eucharistic table, the grains of wheat, that is, the believers—ground by trials—become in the fire of the Spirit, like the bread they receive, a single loaf which is Christ assuming in his communion the whole of reconciled humankind: "It is your own mystery which is on the table of the Lord . . . He has consecrated on his table

---

[54] See Augustine, *Sermon* 71.20, 33, in Hill, 3:258, 266. See already Cyprian, *On the Lord's Prayer* 23.

the mystery of our peace and our unity." Therefore, live in communion as brothers and sisters . . . there resides your Christian identity.

2. If we have lingered over Augustine's intuition and his way of joining Eucharist and church, it is because, in our opinion, it represents the most profound vision of ecclesiology in the West at a time it has not yet cut itself off from the East. Isaac of Stella (ca. 1150), Thomas Aquinas (in 1274), whose theology will be preserved by his Dominican family, Cajetan (at the time of the Reformation) are the proofs that this vision will persist in the West even when currents coming from very different directions will gain favor. Therefore, when in the spirit of Vatican II and the theological renewal that prepared it, the Latin church again places the accent on the ecclesiology of communion, it rejoins its past and the vision that was prevalent at the time of what is called the undivided church. One cannot say that it "capitulates before the Eastern tradition" or that "it is inspired more by Afanasieff and the *Sobornost* of Khomiakoff and the Russian theologians who have emigrated [to the West] than by its own doctors."[55]

It is clearly evident that in the first centuries, the West does not define the church first of all by its hierarchical structure. It places this structure—whose necessity it maintains and connects with the divine will—at the service of the inner communion of grace scrutinized on the basis of Augustine's theology.[56] For the West, the church is the

---

[55] This is the criticism which certain people have directed towards our own research in this domain, a censure that to us seems based on a lack of familiarity with the great tradition. [Sobornost: "In modern Russian theology it denotes a unity of many persons within the organic fellowship of the Church, each person maintaining his full freedom and personal integrity." Elizabeth A. Livingstone, ed., *The Concise Oxford Dictionary of the Christian Church* (New York: Oxford University, 1977) 470. Ed.].

[56] In order to study further what we have presented only too briefly, readers may consult, besides the *Bibliothèque augustinienne* (Paris: Desclée, De Brouwer (1936–), older books such as Gaston Lecordier, *La doctrine de l'Eucharistie chez saint Augustin* (Paris, Gabalda, 1930); Augustine, *Augustini textus eucharistici selecti*, ed. Hugo Lang, Florilegium patristicum 25 (Bonn: Hanstein, 1933); P. Bertocchi, *Il simbolismo ecclesiologico della Eucaristia in Sant' Agostino* (Bergamo, 1937). See also Thomas Camelot, "L'Eucharistie mystère d'unité selon saint Augustin," *La Vie Spirituelle* 73 (1945) 301–17; Camelot, "Réalisme et symbolisme dans la doctrine eucharistique de saint Augustin," *RSPT* 31 (1947) 394–410; Camelot, "Sacramentum fidei," in Congrès international augustinien (Paris, 1954), *Augustinus Magister*, 3 vols. (Paris: Études augustiniennes, 1954–1955) 891–96; Charles Journet, "Saint Augustin et

communion which constitutes what Thomas Aquinas will call "the principal effect of the Eucharist," a grace of the Spirit conferred on those entrusted with the ministry to which the Lord had called his apostles. This ministry is essential, necessary. As early as Cyprian, it will be at the heart of ecclesial problems. When in *Lumen Gentium* (Dogmatic Constitution on the Church), Vatican II declares, "The society equipped with hierarchical structures and the mystical body of Christ . . . are not to be thought of as two realities. On the contrary, they form one complex reality comprising a human and a divine element," it does not deny that within this unity there exists an order and that the spiritual and internal dimension has the primacy.[57]

V. THE RITES IN THE EAST

1. What we just found in Augustine, who is the witness par excellence of the thinking of the West when the church was still undivided, we find stated with other emphases in the East during the first centuries. Whether in Antioch or Alexandria, Christians are convinced that if the church is the body of Christ, it owes this to the table of the Lord, where the Spirit is at work. Christians of those regions are equally convinced that the effect of the Eucharist is to establish the faithful in a real *agapē* which is expressed by mutual love and service but has its source in the unique power of the body of Christ—body of reconciliation and redemption—which embraces all. John of Damascus (ca. 750) sums up the thinking of the East in a formula in which the

---

l'Exégèse traditionnelle du 'corpus spirituale,'" in *Augustinus Magister* 879–90; L. J. Van der Lof, "Eucharistie et présence réelle chez saint Augustin," *REA* 10 (1964) 295–304; Wilhelm Gessel, *Eucharistische Gemeinschaft bei Augustinus* (Würzburg: Augustinus-Verlag, 1966); Charles Boyer and M. F. Berrouard, "L'Église communauté d'amour et de vie selon saint Augustin," *Lumen Vitae* 16 (1967) 40–64; Charles Boyer, "L'être sacramentel de l'Eucharistie selon saint Augustin," *NRT* 99 (1977) 702–21; L. Arias, "La Eucaristia signo de la unidad de la Iglesia," *Estudio Augustiniano* 3 (1968) 319–40; Athanase Sage, "L'Eucharistie dans la pensée de saint Augustin," *REA* 15 (1969) 209–40; Bertrand de Margerie, "La doctrine de saint Augustin sur L'Esprit-Saint comme communion et source de communion," *Augustinianum* 12 (1972) 107–19; René Bergeron, "La doctrine eucharistique de l'*Enarr. in Ps 33*, d'Augustin," *REA* 19 (1973) 101–20; Cor Traaets, "The Eucharist and Christian Community: Some Pauline and Augustinian Evidence," *Louvain Studies* 12 (1987) 152–71.

[57] Vatican Council II, *The Basic Sixteen Documents: Constitutions, Decrees, Declarations*, completely rev., trans. in incl. lang., ed. Austin Flannery (Northport, N.Y.: Costello, 1996) no. 8, p. 9.

West will recognize its own faith, "For if the sacrament is in truth a union with Christ and with one another, it gives us unity in every way with all those who receive it with us."[58]

2. It would be easy to demonstrate that although the understanding of the rites of initiation is the same in the two traditions, it has its own overtones in the East. We shall cite only one example—which readers will compare to Augustine's texts—a passage from Didymus the Blind (d. 398), friend of Athanasius and master of Gregory of Nazianzus. Whereas Augustine has the community in view before all else (the fire of the Holy Spirit baking into a single loaf the grains ground and kneaded with the baptismal water), Didymus is more concerned with what happens to the individual, with the new birth of the Christian:

"Because the Holy Spirit is God, it renews us through baptism. . . . John, when he added this word of Christ, 'No one can enter the kingdom of God without being born of water and Spirit,' showed us that this God who gives birth is the Holy Spirit. . . . The baptismal fountain, through the ministry of priests, gives birth to our visible body. But the Spirit of God, invisible to all intellects, baptizes into itself in a spiritual way and causes both our body and our soul to be re-created through being served by the angels.

"For his part, John the Baptist, in accordance with the saying quoted above on the water and the Spirit, literally said when speaking of Christ, 'He will baptize you with the Holy Spirit and fire.' *The human body is similar to a vessel made by the potter: first, it needs to be purified by water; afterwards, it needs to be made solid by a spiritual fire which gives it its perfection. For our 'God is a devouring fire'* [Deut 4:24]. This is the reason it needs to be completed and renewed by the Holy Spirit. *For the spiritual fire is also able to bathe us, and the spiritual water is able to melt us in order to remake us.*"[59]

It is true that when speaking of the Eucharist, the East stresses the ecclesial function of the "fire of the Spirit." As a proof of this we may cite the Easter homily inspired by a text of Hippolytus (3rd century),[60]

---

[58] John of Damascus, *Exposition of the Orthodox Faith* 4.13, in Schaff and Wace, 9:84.

[59] Didymus the Blind, *On the Trinity* 2.12, in *PG* 39:672–73.

[60] Pierre Nautin, ed. and trans., *Homélies pascales*, vol. 1: *Une homelie inspirée du Traité sur la Paque d'Hippolyte*, SC 27 (1950).

often close to Gaudentius of Brescia (whom we have quoted)[61] but decidedly more Eastern:

"Such are for us the fare of the sacred feast, such is our spiritual banquet, such are our immortal food and our immortal delights. Having eaten the bread come down from heaven and having drunk the cup of gladness, *the bubbling and hot chalice, the blood warmed from above by the heat of the Spirit, let us say first, by recalling the beginning, what the law and the economy of the law are,* for thus we shall know by comparison what the Word and the freedom of the Word are."[62]

This bubbling attributed to the Spirit is suggested in the Eastern rite of the *Zeon* (*teplota* in Slavonic): after the Our Father, the deacon pours a little boiling water into the chalice while saying, "fervor of the faith filled with the Holy Spirit." By this formula, close to Eucharistic Prayer 3 of the Latin liturgy,[63]

"the accent is placed on the presence of the Spirit in the sacrament of the body and blood of Christ in order to show that the effect of the Eucharist is to communicate the Spirit to the Church, this Spirit that 'has spoken through the prophets' (creed of Nicaea-Constantinople) and in all the Scriptures, and that now 'causes them to be understood'" (Hippolytus).[64]

Thus, the link between the Eucharist and the whole economy of salvation is symbolically affirmed. For its part, the West underlines this link by reading the Law and the Prophets in the first part of the synaxis, by mentioning Abel and Abraham in the Roman Canon, and sometimes—as in the local church of Venice—by celebrating the saints of the Old Covenant. In the eucharistic chalice, the *martyria* (witness) of the people of God, continuing into that of its Christ where it finds its fulfillment *(teleiōsis)*, joins the synaxis of the local church. But instead of surveying the variations in the liturgies, it is probably more worthwhile to present, as we have done for the Western tradition, the

[61] Ibid., 49–51, 56–57.

[62] Ibid., no. 8, pp. 131–33.

[63] The Latin text says, "qui Corpore et Sanguine Filii tui reficimur, Spiritu ejus Sancto repleti" (Grant that we, who are nourished by his body and blood, may be filled with his Holy Spirit. . . .)

[64] Nautin, *Homélies pascales,* 68.

visions that dominate the Eastern tradition at the time of the undivided church.

VI. JOHN CHRYSOSTOM,
WITNESS OF THE CHURCH OF ANTIOCH

In Antioch, the most prominent witness to the belief in an intrinsic link between Eucharist and church is John Chrysostom (d. 407), patriarch of Constantinople, a fiery preacher not shy about using strong language to express his intuitions. Thus, he brings to this doctrine a special emphasis.

According to Chrysostom, the Eucharist effects much more than a connection between Christ and the faithful. It establishes a close union where all are one *unit*. He has Christ pronouncing the following statement:

"I am chewed, ground into bits, so that the mixing, the blending, the union may be more complete. *Things united remain themselves, but I am interwoven with you. I want no more division between us. I want both of us to be one.*"[65]

In their communal participation in the bread of Christ, believers together become "this same thing" in Christ:

"Why does Paul add 'that we break' [1 Cor 10:16]? For even though we see this done in the Eucharist, yet it was not so on the cross; on the contrary, 'None of his bones shall be broken' [John 19:36]. But what he did not suffer on the cross, he allows for your sake in the oblation and lets himself be broken so that he may fill everyone.

"Furthermore, because Paul said, 'a communion of the body' [1 Cor 10:16, KJV] and because those who communicate are distinct from the one on whom they communicate, he removed even this seemingly small difference. Having said, 'a communion of the body,' he tried to say something more intimate; and so he added, 'Because there is one bread, we who are many are one body' [1 Cor 10:17]. This is like saying, 'Why do I speak of communion? We are that very body.' What is the bread? The body of Christ. Not many bodies, one body. Just as the bread is made of many grains, but so united that the single grains disappear, although they indeed exist but without their differences being

---

[65] John Chrysostom, *Homilies on 1 Timothy* 15, in Schaff, 13:464.

seen because of their cohering, so we cohere with one another and with Christ. You do not eat one body, and your neighbor another; we all eat the same body. For this reason, Paul adds, 'We all partake of the one bread' [1 Cor 10:17]. Now if we are all nourished by the same and all become the same, why do we all not witness to the same love, and in this respect also become one?"

All this comes from Christ, as a gift of the absoluteness of his grace:

"'The bread which we break, is it not the communion of the body of Christ?' [1 Cor 10:16, KJV]. Why did he not say 'participation'? Because he wanted to express something more and to point out how close the union was: we communicate not only by participating and partaking but also by being united. For as that body is united to Christ, so are we united to him by this bread."[66]

But this close union is nothing else than the state of belonging to the church:

"Let us cleave to [Christ, our foundation], as a branch to the vine, *and let nothing come between us and Christ. If there is any separation, we immediately perish. For the branch lives because it draws in nourishment through its attachment to the vine, and the building stands because it is cemented together; if it stands apart it perishes, having nothing under it. Let us not merely keep hold of Christ. Let us be cemented to him; if we stand apart, we perish.* For it is said, 'Behold, they that remove themselves far from you shall perish' [Ps 72:27, LXX]. Let us cleave to him then, let us cleave to him by our works. 'They who have my commandments and keep them [abide in me]' [John 14:21]. Indeed, he depicts our union with him in many ways. Thus, he is the head, we are the body. *Can there be any empty space between the head and the body? He is the foundation, we are the building; he the vine, we the branches; he the bridegroom, we the bride; he the shepherd, we the sheep; he the way, we the travellers; we the temple, he the indweller; he the heir, we the coheirs; he the life, we the living; he the resurrection, we those who rise again; he the light, we the enlightened.* All these express unity, and they allow not even the smallest empty space. For those who separate themselves just a little bit will continue to widen the gap until they are very far away. It is the same with the

---

[66] John Chrysostom, *Homilies on 1 Corinthians* 24.16-17, in Schaff, 12:139–40.

body: if it receives even a small wound from a sword, it dies. And a building: if there is even a narrow crack, it falls into decay. And a branch: if it is slightly cut off from the root, it will wither. So this trifle is no trifle. It is practically everything."[67]

Chrysostom looks at the mystery of this unity by the light of the gospel of reconciliation, and in this he is without compare. He brings to the theology of the Eucharist and the church a specific note, rarely emphasized: the sacrament shows that communion with Christ renders null and void any distinction of race, dignity, or social status. In Christ, all are equal. At the baptismal font and at the eucharistic table, there no longer exists any hierarchy, any preferential treatment. In view of the mores of the time, this is an astonishing, a quasi-revolutionary position:

"Finally, here is something admirable and unbelievable. Every distinction, every difference in status are here swept away. If some are endowed with worldly honors or the splendor of riches, if they take pride in their being highborn or having glory in this present life, here they are placed on the same footing as beggars and those in rags or, as it happens, the blind and crippled. And they are not indignant over this because they know that none of these distinctions apply in the spiritual realities where what counts is only the good disposition of the soul."[68]

Moreover, in Constantinople itself,

"the emperor—wearing the diadem and clad in purple garments, in charge of the government of the world—as well as the poor, sitting and begging for alms, partake of one table."[69]

And in case one thinks an exception might be made during the paschal night, this would not go without creating problems:

"At the great feast of Easter, the emperor was accustomed to receive communion in the holy of holies; Pulcheria desired [the same privi-

---

[67] Ibid., 8.11, in Schaff, 12:47.
[68] John Chrysostom, *Baptismal Homily* 2.13., in Jean Chrysostome, *Huit catéchèses baptismales inédites,* 2nd ed., ed. and trans. Antoine Wenger, SC 50 (1970) 140.
[69] John Chrysostom, *On the Resurrection of Our Lord Jesus Christ* 3, in PG 50:437.

lege] and convinced Bishop Sisinnius, who allowed her to receive communion with the emperor in the holy of holies. Nestorius did not permit this, and one day when, according to custom, she was going to the holy of holies, Nestorius saw her and inquired what this meant; Peter the archdeacon explained the situation. Nestorius ran, met her at the door of the holy of holies, stopped her, and forbade her to enter."[70]

This equality of all at the sacraments of baptism and Eucharist is for Chrysostom pregnant with implications and meaning:

"In the church, there is no difference between slave and free, foreigner and citizen, old and young, commoner and prince, woman and man. But man or woman, whatever the age or social class, enters the fountain of baptismal water in the same way. *The* basileus *(emperor) as well as the poor receive the same purification. This is the greatest sign of nobility characterizing the church: we initiate the beggar into Christ in the same way as the one who holds the scepter in his hands."* [71]

2. However, there exists a nuance in this equality. Precisely because of what it accomplishes in the Eucharist, the church has a preference for the poorest and neediest.[72] Indeed, in the eucharistic memorial, Christ is both the victim and the altar. The sacrifice is offered on the altar. Now, for the church on its journey, the one altar of the cross is refracted, as it were, into two closely connected altars, with the one being only the sacrament of the other. There is the stone altar and there is the ecclesial body of Christ:

"This altar is made of Christ's members themselves, and the body of the Lord becomes your altar. Venerate it: you sacrifice the victim on the flesh of the Lord. This altar is more awesome than the one we use here, not just more than the one used in ancient times [in the Old Testament]. No, do not object. This altar is awesome because of the sacrifice laid upon it; that, the one made of alms, is even more so, not just because of the alms, but because it is the very sacrifice which makes the other awesome. Again, this altar, only stone, becomes holy because Christ's body touches it, but that is holy because it is

[70] This is a quotation from the letter of Constantinople translated by François Nau in an appendix to Nestorius, *Le livre d'Héraclite de Damas,* trans. and ed. François Nau (Paris: Letouzey, 1910) 364.

[71] John Chrysostom, *Homily on 1 Corinthians 10:1,* in *PG* 51:247.

[72] John Chrysostom, *Homily on Easter, Against Drunkenness,* in *PG* 50:437.

itself Christ's body. So that is more awesome, sisters and brothers, than the one you are standing beside.

"What then is Aaron in comparison to these things, or his crown or his bells or the Holy of Holies? From now on, what need do we have to make any comparison with Aaron's altar *when compared with our altar itself, the one made of alms has been shown to be so glorious? You indeed honor this altar because it receives Christ's body. But those who are themselves the body of Christ you treat with contempt and ignore as they die. You can see that altar everywhere, lying in the lanes and market places, and every hour of the day you can sacrifice upon it; for there too is sacrifice performed. And as the priest stands invoking the Spirit, so you also invoke the Spirit, not by speech but by deeds because nothing so kindles and sustains the fire of the Spirit as this oil poured out in abundance."*[73]

The Eucharist, which creates the ecclesial body, "builds" the altar on which the sacrifice that pleases God is celebrated. The poor are the most sacred part of the altar "made" by the Eucharist. John Chrysostom does not say—as Augustine does in the text which we know from *The City of God*—that at the sacrifice of the altar, the "sacrifices" of *agapē*, the actions done in service to the poor and the help given to others are taken into the sacrifice of Christ and, in it, are offered to the Father. He prefers to state that the same sacrifice of the one Christ is celebrated on the two altars in a necessarily conjoined way. For the body of the paschal sacrifice is present on the stone altar in order to form the ecclesial body. In this ecclesial body, Christ lives in his members. He is served and honored (according to Matthew 25:32-46) by the "good deeds" which are "pleasing to God" (Heb 13:16). On the altar of the ecclesial body, and especially on the most worthy part, which is the poor, Christ himself becomes the object of the liturgy of the sacrifice. Commenting on Matthew, Chrysostom will declare:

"You want to honor Christ's body? Then do not neglect him when he is naked. Do not honor him here with silk garments while you leave him outside perishing from cold and nakedness. For he who said, 'This is my body,' and by his word confirmed the fact, also said, 'For I was hungry and you gave me no food,' and, 'Just as you did not do it to one of the least of these, you did not do it to me' (Matt 25:42, 45). Here, the body of Christ needs no clothing, but pure souls; there, it needs great solicitude.

[73] John Chrysostom, *Homilies on 2 Corinthians* 20, in Schaff, 12:374.

"Let us learn, then, to be conscientious in life and to honor Christ as he himself desires. For the honor most pleasing to him is what he wants, not what we think is best. Peter also thought he honored Christ by forbidding him to wash his feet; however, it was not an honor, but completely the contrary. And so honor him with the honor he has decreed, spending your wealth on the poor. For God has no need of golden vessels, but of golden souls.

"I say these things, not forbidding you to make such offerings, but requiring you to give alms along with them, before them. For indeed, he accepts the former, but the latter much more. In the one, the offerer alone benefits, but in the other, the receiver as well. Here the act seems to be grounds for ostentation, but there all is mercifulness and love for humanity.

"What profit is there if Christ's table is set with golden cups but he dies from hunger? First feed him and relieve his hunger; then abundantly deck out his table also. Do you make him a cup of gold and not give him a cup of cold water? What is the profit? Do you cover his table with cloths glittering with gold and not give him even necessary clothing? What good comes from that? Tell me, if you see him lacking necessary food and neglect to alleviate his hunger while you first set his table with silver, is he going to thank you rather than be indignant? Again, if you see him wrapped in rags and stiff with cold and neglect to give him a coat while you build golden columns, saying you were doing it to honor him, is he not going to say that you are mocking him and consider it a supreme insult?

"Remember this also in regard to Christ, he is going about, a wanderer, a stranger, needing a roof to shelter him, and you neglect to welcome him while you deck out a pavement and walls and the capitals of columns, and you hang lamps from silver chains, but you will not even look at him chained in prison. I say these things, not forbidding generosity in these matters, but admonishing you to do those other works together with these, or rather even before these. No one was ever blamed for not doing these, but for neglecting those, hell is threatened, and unquenchable fire and punishment by evil spirits. Therefore, do not ignore your sisters and brothers in distress while you adorn Christ's house, for they are more a temple than the other."[74]

---

[74] John Chrysostom, *Homilies on the Gospel of Matthew* 50.4-5, in Schaff 10:313.

Accordingly, the liturgy of the Eucharist and the liturgy of service to the poor (a necessary part of the sacrifice of the holy life) are the celebration of one and the same sacrifice. But the liturgy of the poor actualizes in concrete actions what the synaxis signifies. Chrysostom sometimes seems to assert—beyond certain very strong oratorical locutions—that the union with Christ effected by the eucharistic communion remains fruitless if it does not result in concern for the poor and does not translate the equality "before God" shown at the table of the Lord into actual behavior. The Eucharist is the sacrament that renders the faithful so completely "one with Christ" that they must reach the point where they make their own, and relieve as if it were their own, the suffering of the whole body. So the Eucharist implies a demand to which the response of the community as a whole and the individual members of the faithful is always unequal. And Chrysostom vehemently berates the mediocrity of his audience.

3. John Chrysostom's vision is shared by all his church. It is significant that it is found also in a passage of Nestorius (patriarch of Constantinople, who was deposed by the council of Ephesus in 431 and died about 450). Leaving aside the traces of a deviant christology which certain commentators detect in it,[75] one sees the same line of thought as in Augustine and Chrysostom.

"Are we not all *a single body in a single thing? Indeed, all of us receive this same bread by which he makes us partakers of the same blood and the same flesh,* which are of the same nature, and *partakers with him through resurrection from the dead and through immortality. We are his in the same way the bread is his body; in truth, in the same way the bread is one, in the same way all of us are one body because all of us receive that one bread.*

"On this point: if in Christ the essence of the flesh has been changed into divinity, we also are changed into the essence of God the Word, for we are a single compound and a single Body.

"We have thus been changed into his flesh and we are his body. From now on we are no longer the body and blood of humanity, but Christ's own body. *For the bread is one, and this is why all of us are a single body, because we are the body of Christ;* in truth, you are the body of Christ and his members, each one for his or her part. . . . Indeed, if

---

[75] Thus Martin Jugie, *Nestorius et la Controverse nestorienne,* Bibliothèque de théologie historique (Paris: Beauchesne, 1912) 252–70.

all of us do not come from the One, it is right that we are called neither his brothers nor sisters nor his children and that we are neither his bread nor his body; but if all of this really belongs to Christ, we are his body and consubstantial with him because we are also what the essence of his body is."[76]

VII. CYRIL, WITNESS OF THE CHURCH OF ALEXANDRIA

1. In Alexandria at the same period, Cyril also uses realistic expressions to characterize the close communion of Christians with Christ and their communion with one another as effected by the Eucharist. Of course, in Cyril's case, one has to deal with a christology using the difficult concept of the assumption of human nature *as such* into Christ.[77] However, this in no way impairs the acuity of his understanding of the sacrament of the holy eulogy (consecrated bread).[78] He sees there the locus of the union with Christ.

Several of his statements are classic and are part of the undivided church's common treasury of the tradition. Thus, two texts often quoted and reminiscent of Augustine and Chrysostom. One of them speaks of being one body:

"Because we participate in the Spirit, we are united with the savior of all and with one another. We thus become one body: 'because there is one bread, we who are many are one body, for we all partake of the one bread.' The body of Christ which is in us ties us into one since it is in no way divided."[79]

The commentary on John's Gospel is perhaps more clearly typical of Cyril's theological intuition with its various overtones:

"We are all one, in the Father, the Son, and the Holy Spirit. I say that we are one by sharing the same nature (it is useful to repeat what has

[76] Nestorius, *Livre d'Héraclite,* 29–30.

[77] See the important introduction of Georges-Matthieu de Durand to Cyril of Alexandria, *Deux dialogues christologiques,* trans. and ed. G.-M. de Durand, SC 97 (1964) especially 93–98.

[78] See ibid., 96–97; Henry Chadwick, "Eucharist and Christology in the Nestorian Controversy," *JST* 2 (1951) 145–64; J. Mahé, "L'Eucharistie d'après saint Cyrille d'Alexandrie," *RHE* 8 (1907) 677–96, which remains the basic work; Mahé, "La sanctification d'après saint Cyrille d'Alexandrie," *RHE* 10 (1909) 30–40, 469–92; Jean-Marie-Roger Tillard, *The Eucharist: Pasch of God's People,* trans. Dennis L. Wienk (Staten Island: Alba House, 1967).

[79] Cyril of Alexandria, *Against Nestorius* 4, in *PG* 76:193; see ibid., 3, in *PG* 76:125–29.

already been said), by the formation acquired through piety, and by the communion of the holy flesh of Christ and by the communion of the one Holy Spirit, as has already been said."[80]

2. This union with Christ is what Paul calls the body of reconciliation, the temple of God, therefore the church, fruit of the incarnation (the assumption of human nature into the Word) and of the cross:

"We were all in Christ, and the corporate person of humankind is formed again in him. This is why he was called the second Adam, since he communicates to the whole of nature all the riches of happiness and glory in the same way the first Adam had brought on us the curses of corruption and disgrace.

"Therefore, through one person, the Word has dwelt among us. One person having been constituted 'Son of God in power, according to the spirit of holiness' [Rom 1:4], his dignity is communicated to the whole human race so that through one of us, this word reaches us also: 'I say, you are gods, children of the Most High, all of you' [Ps 82:6]. . . . He has dwelt among us, he who, by nature, is Son of God, so that, through his Spirit, we are able to cry 'Abba, Father.' In truth, the Word dwells in all, in the unique temple he has taken for us and from us so that, according to Saint Paul, having all of us in himself, he may reconcile all of us in one body, with God his Father" [see Eph 2:16].[81]

Through the Eucharist, the "in Christ" reaches a mysterious reality, which Cyril strives to make understandable through a very simple image, that of fusion, of mixture. For,

"our teaching does not deny that we are spiritually united with Christ by sentiments of perfect charity, a true and unshakable faith, the love of virtue, and the sincerity of our convictions. We too declare that this is perfectly correct. However, if it is said that with Christ we have no connection involving the flesh, we can prove that this is not in conformity with Holy Scripture. Then let our interrogators tell us what is the raison d'être and power of the mystical eulogy. Why does it come into us? Is it not to bring Christ into us, bodily, through the participation in and the communion of his holy flesh? . . . We become one body with him through the reception of the mystical eulogy and we are made

---

[80] Cyril of Alexandria, *On John* 11.11, in *PG* 74:561.
[81] Ibid., 12.1, in *PG* 74:608–9.

one body with him, as were the holy apostles. Has not Christ said that their members, or rather, our members, the members of all of us, were his? Indeed, it is written, 'Do you not know that your bodies are members of Christ?' [1 Cor 6:15]. And the Savior says, 'Those who eat my flesh and drink my blood abide in me, and I in them' [John 6:56]. We must note here that Christ is not speaking of being in us by an affective relationship, but by a physical [*physikēn*] participation. If someone should fashion two pieces of wax into one by melting them in the heat of fire, she or he would reduce these two pieces into one; in the same way, through the reception of the body of Christ and the precious blood, he is in us and we are united with him. What was born corruptible could be vivified only by being bodily mixed with the body of life itself, that is, the Only-begotten. If you do not want to be persuaded by my words, at least believe Christ, who proclaims, 'Whoever eats of this bread will live forever' [John 6:51]. In truth, eternal life is the flesh of life, that is, the flesh of the only Son."[82]

Elsewhere, he has recourse to biblical images:

"Saint Paul writes, 'A little yeast leavens the whole batch of dough' [1 Cor 5:6]. Likewise, a very small eulogy causes our entire body to rise. It fills it with its own energy. Thus, Christ comes into us and we, for our part, come into him. And can we not say in truth that the leaven is in the whole mass and that, likewise, the whole mass is absorbed by the leaven?"[83]

Such a union leads to eternal life. Here again Cyril knows how to find the appropriate image:

"It is unthinkable that the one who is life by nature does not entirely triumph over corruption and vanquish death. This is why, even though death—which invaded us on account of sin—has the power to subject our body to corruption, we will truly rise because Christ comes into us by his flesh. It would be unbelievable, or rather impossible, that life should not vivify those into whom it comes. In the same way one covers a spark with a heap of straw in order to preserve the seed of the fire, so in us, our Lord Jesus Christ, *by his flesh*, hides life in

[82] Ibid., 10.2, in *PG* 74:341–44.
[83] Ibid., 4.6, in *PG* 73:584.

the innermost part of our being. He deposits it as a germ of immortality which will consume the corruption that is in us."[84]

But this communion with Christ, which carries people and their destinies into the power of the eucharistic body, fuses the communicants together into an unbreakable unity; it makes them into an essentially ecclesial body. Cyril often comes back to this. One feels that for him this certitude is preeminent, and pregnant with implications. What is at stake is the concrete life of the church:

"Whereas we are divided into separate individuals, one Peter, the other Paul, or Thomas, or Matthew, we have become one body in Christ, nourished by one flesh and stamped with the seal of unity by the one Holy Spirit, and since Christ is indivisible—one cannot in fact divide him in any way—in him we are all one. Thus he spoke to his Father, 'That they may be one, as we are one' [John 17:11, 22]. Consider how we are one in Christ and the Holy Spirit, according both to the body and to the spirit. We must therefore blame those who, thinking in another way, understand poorly what has been written for our sake."[85]

Such seems to be the primary reason d'être of the Eucharist, "Through his sacred flesh, to make of all one life in him":

"In order to unite us also, to melt us into unity with God and among ourselves while we are separated into distinct personalities, the only Son has invented a way that he found in his wisdom, according to the Father's design. Indeed, through one body, his own body, he blesses his faithful in the mystical communion, making them one body with him and among themselves.

"Who now could separate, deprive of their physical unity, those who have been joined together in unity in Christ, by means of his body, one and holy? For if all of us eat the one bread, all of us form one body. Division cannot exist in Christ. Because of this, the church is called the body of Christ and we are called his members, each one for his or her part, as Saint Paul teaches. Since all of us are united to the one Christ through his holy body, since all of us receive it, one and

[84] Ibid., 4.2, in *PG* 73:581; see also ibid., 4.3, in *PG* 73:601; 10.2, in *PG* 74:342.
[85] Cyril of Alexandria, *Dialogue on the Holy Trinity* 1, in *PG* 75:697.

76

indivisible, into our own bodies, we must consider our members as belonging to him more than to us."[86]

The force and cohesion of this unity *(henōsis)* come from Christ, himself the mystery of unity:

"Since we are all one body in Christ one with another, and not only one with another, but also with him who comes into us by his flesh, how could we not be one, all of us, in one another and in Christ? Christ is indeed the bond of unity because he is one and the same, God and human being."[87]

The life of the church, as it is presented in Ephesians, has its foundation here and has its charter of communion here. For life according to the Spirit is inseparable from the quasi-physical union that the Eucharist establishes between believers:

"Having received into ourselves the one Spirit, that is to say, the Holy Spirit, we are by the same token blended together and with God. Of course we are distinct from one another, and the Spirit of the Father and the Son dwells in each of us. However, this Spirit is one and indivisible. As a consequence, the Spirit gathers into unity, by itself, numerous and distinct spirits, making them one spirit in itself. I think that as the power of the holy flesh makes those who receive it one body among themselves, so the one Spirit that comes to dwell in all leads them all to spiritual unity. In this regard, Paul declares, '[Bear] with one another in love, [make] every effort to maintain the unity of the Spirit in the bond of peace. There is one body and one Spirit, just as you were called to the one hope of your calling, one Lord, one faith, one baptism, one God and Father of all, who is above all and through all and in all' [Eph 4:2-6]. In truth, if the one Spirit of God resides in us all, the one Father of all will be God in us and through the Son will lead those who have a share in the Spirit into unity among themselves and with God."[88]

---

[86] Cyril of Alexandria, *On John* 11.11, in *PG* 74:560.

[87] Ibid.

[88] Ibid., 561. See also ibid., 3, in *PG* 73:520; 4.2, in *PG* 73:561; 7.1–8.1, in *PG* 73:584; 11.6, in *PG* 74:488; *Against Nestorius* 4, in *PG* 76:197; *That Christ Is One*, in *PG* 65:1273, 1360. The *sensus fidei* (the insight of faith) is established there: "The Word, the only Son of the Father, when he gives the saints the Spirit, places in them a

3. Cyril thus explains the source and nature of the ecclesial unity, perhaps better than Augustine and John Chrysostom. This source is no other than Christ in his body as the New Adam. This nature is essentially christological. In no way are we speaking of a pure and simple agreement of minds, or even of a pure and simple union of charity. The Eucharist connects the church by connecting it with Christ in what Cyril calls a physical union, probably meaning the communion of being which the presence of the eucharistic body in the spiritual and corporeal reality of the baptized effects. Their human nature, inherited from the first Adam, is then taken up (body and soul) into that of the second Adam. This seizing of the individual *phusis* (nature) by the eucharistic flesh of the second Adam is no simple passing event, in spite of the short duration of the synaxis. For the body of Christ is given with the Spirit and this is the energy which persists after the contact. Another image of Cyril's explains:

"By its nature, water is cold, but poured into a vessel and placed over the fire, it almost forgets its own nature and is taken up into the energy of the element that overcomes it. The same happens to us. Although corruptible with regard to the nature of our flesh, we let go of our own weakness by being mixed with the true life and are restored into what is proper to this eulogy, that is to say, life. For it was necessary, not only that the soul be re-created by the Spirit in view of a new life, but also that our heavy and earthly body be sanctified by a participation more tangible and more akin to it and thus be called to incorruptibility."[89]

Eucharistic communion leaves in the flesh of believers the imprint of the flesh of Christ, with the Spirit. The church of God is born from this imprint left in all believers.

VIII. THE FAITH OF THE TRADITION

By quoting the most significant texts from three Fathers of the Church representing three different traditions—all belonging to the

---

kinship, as it were, with his nature, especially if they are united to him through faith and perfect holiness. He feeds them, increases their piety, develops in them the knowledge of all virtue and all kindness" (Commentary on the allegory of the vine, in *On John* 10.2, in *PG* 74:344).

[89] Cyril of Alexandria, *On John* 4.2, in *PG* 73:577–80.

still undivided church of the fifth century—we proposed to illustrate the universal theological conviction that Eucharist and church are closely linked. The fundamental convergences of those texts, enriched by the specific accents proper to each writer, enable us to declare that from the very beginning, the tradition of the first centuries sees the church as the communion of the baptized with the Father and with one another in Christ's (the new Adam's) body of reconciliation given at the eucharistic table.

1. Everything is subordinated to this communion, in particular the hierarchical structure. Its necessity is beyond all doubt; it is unceasingly present in the ecclesial consciousness. But it is never regarded as primary—Thomas Aquinas will say "as *res*"—that is, as the ultimate reality God had in view in the eternal plan when the Son was sent. The structure belongs with the church on its journey, whereas the principal effect of the Eucharist is already eschatological. This explains why even here on earth, the institution does not have full mastery over the communion of grace, in relation to which it is only the servant of Christ in the power of the Spirit. The Donatist dispute gave Augustine the opportunity to become aware of this. Besides, if in the synaxis and the life of the local church, the bishop represents either the Father or Christ surrounded by his apostles, it is obvious that in the heavenly liturgy, on which Augustine, Chrysostom, and Cyril train their gaze, the Father and Christ need no representation. The ecclesial hierarchy —it is its grandeur and its necessity—belongs to the fabric of the church on its journey as sacrament of the very source of the communion. This alone defines the church of God, from the righteous Abel on and into eternity. This patristic vision of what *Lumen Gentium* will call "the society equipped with hierarchical structures" seems crucial to us. While the hierarchy belongs with the sacrament, the communion effected by the Eucharist is already *res eschatologica* (eschatological reality).

2. If everything is subordinated to the communion which the Eucharist realizes, at the same time, everything proceeds from it. The nature of the church is to be communion. For Augustine, Chrysostom, and Cyril, the bread and the cup are the focus of an evangelical communion intended to be realized by gestures, attitudes, feelings of solidarity day in and day out. The members of Christ and the Christian communities among themselves *ought* to live by being *in truth* "one heart and one soul," one body animated by one *agapē*. Both East and West

79

specify that here service to the poor and little ones has a place of honor. By virtue of the Eucharist, the church is compelled to accomplish what Chrysostom described as the Liturgy of the Lord in his suffering members; after all, the church enters the Eucharist in the power of the One whose commitment to the weak surely brought about his condemnation and death. And for his part, Augustine showed that by the celebration of the sacrament of the altar, these "sacrifices" of ecclesial charity pass, as it were, into the sacrifice of Christ in order to glorify the Father through him, with him, and in him. The Eucharist is by its very nature *sacramentum Ecclesiae* (the sacrament of the church), of the church in act of communion. Such is the answer of the Father to the prayer of the epiclesis.

The effect of the Eucharist in the personal lives of the faithful is not denied in all we have said. We deliberately quoted texts from Augustine, Chrysostom, and Cyril showing the depth of the personal union the Eucharist creates between every believer and the Lord Jesus Christ and emphasizing that the strength of the communal bonds has its origin in this personal union. Besides, we have highlighted the importance which the three of them accord to the Spirit. For them, the Eucharist confers the bond of the ecclesial body, the Holy Spirit, within the glorified body of the Lord. This is why the effect of the bread of life in the life of each Christian is communion with the Lord inasmuch as each Christian is united with all of her or his sisters and brothers, and thus communion in the Spirit with all the other members. Both the East and the West do not explain this connection between the personal and the ecclesial in the same way. However, East and West are unanimous not only in the affirmation of this connection but also in the conviction that it is the principal effect of the Eucharist. That the Eastern anaphoras attest to this either in the middle of the epiclesis (prayer to the Father that the Spirit may be sent) or in the account of the institution is no accident. In the Eucharist (where, in the vitality of baptismal rebirth, the body of the Lord in the Spirit grasps the faithful) the faithful receive the power to *fully* live the state of salvation, as we discovered in the preceding chapter: there is no salvation without relation to others.

About 425, therefore at the same period, Theodore of Mopsuestia said this in Antioch in a way that has never been equalled:

"The bishop asks . . . that the grace of the Holy Spirit may come down on all those who are gathered, so that as they have been made whole by a new birth into one body, *they may now be strengthened as one body by communion in the body of Our Lord; that in concord, peace, and zeal for the good, they may succeed in becoming one, so that all of us, thus looking to God with pure hearts, may not receive participation in the Holy Spirit in a way deserving punishment for being divided in our opinions and prone to controversies, quarrels, envy, jealousy, and contempt for good morals.* But that we may show ourselves worthy to receive the Holy Spirit because we live *in concord, peace, and zeal for the good* and with pure hearts turn the eyes of our souls to God. *Thus, in our communion, we shall be united with the holy mysteries, and through this communion, we shall be joined to our head, Christ Our Lord, whose body we believe we are and through whom we obtain communion with the divine nature."*[90]

3. Augustine, Chrysostom, and Cyril live in three different regions. Their traditions are not identical. Even their vision of Christ does not emphasize the same points, although nothing touching the totality of the mystery of the Lord Jesus and his work is negated by any part of these three traditions. Their ritual liturgical formulations differ. In a word, the three belong to diverse local churches, each of which possesses its own theology, its own organization, its own spirit, its own discipline, its own customs, its own problems. The Eucharist which each of these churches celebrates unites, in the communion with Christ and the Spirit, primarily men and women from its own portion of humankind. It reaches them in what preexists it, that is, the solidarity, culture, popular mores, human soil which create a unit, a city, a community characterized by specific traits. The Eucharist makes of this community the body of Christ in which the wound of every human community is healed in the communion of grace and holiness which the Spirit creates. The Eucharist cements first of all the local church.

Into its own human soil, each of the local churches thus "receives" the heritage of the apostolic church, and through the Spirit, this heritage becomes its own possession. Where the Eucharist is, there is the church with everything that makes it the body of Christ in this specific place. Let us stress (as Chrysostom does) that the presence of poor and rich, slaves and emperor, women and men, pagans and Jews, reconciled around the table of the Lord, shows that the church is *for all,* therefore

---

[90] Theodore of Mopsuestia, *Homily 2 on the Mass (Hom. 16.13),* in *Les Homélies catéchétiques de Théodore de Mopsueste,* trans. Raymond Tonneau and Robert Devresse, Studi e testi 145 (Rome: Vatican City, 1949) 555.

catholic, even at that level. But because, despite the diversity, each of the local churches—Hippo, Antioch, Alexandria, but also Gaul and Rome—"recognizes" in the synaxis of the others the same identical features of the body of Christ in their integrity and authenticity, these local churches know themselves to be one body extending over all the world in the communion of one Spirit, one faith, one baptism, one Eucharist, one life. Thus, the Eucharist joins the local churches together.

The catholicity of the church is not limited to the totality of people taken individually. The church is also the communion between all the human communities reconciled "in Christ," with their riches and their lacks, their histories and their projects. In a word, it is the new humanity, in which the immense variety of the creative work of God and the developments which the human genius adds to it are part of the vast mystery of *agapē* springing forth from the heart of God. Such is the amplitude of the catholicity of the church. It gathers into the communion of the Spirit the church *which is* in Hippo, in Constantinople, in Alexandria, in Lyons, in Milan, in Antioch, in Rome. It is eucharistic. For the flesh of the universal church is that of the body given, celebrated, and gathered at the table of the Lord. Now, one understands why.

4. This is probably an ideal view, like the one outlined in the accounts of Acts. Augustine attests to it with his notion of the *corpus permixtum* ["at present, Christ's body is, as it were, mixed on the threshing floor."][91] Chrysostom constantly upbraids his community because of the contradiction existing between what they celebrate and what they live. The ecclesiology of communion, based on the meaning of the Eucharist, is an exacting ecclesiology. It highlights the grandeur of God's work and urges the human heart to rouse itself from its torpor and sin because it knows indeed the weakness of believers, the weight of their spiritual indigence, the banality of their witness, the forces that undermine solidarity between sisters and brothers. This is an ecclesiology which neither demands heroism at any cost nor condones mediocrity: it is the ecclesiology of grace, grace both free and exacting, grace often betrayed.

[91] See Augustine, *Homilies on John* 27.11 and 28.11, in Schaff 7:178 and 183; *On Christian Doctrine* 3.32.45, in Schaff, 2:569; *Sermon* 223.2, in Hill, 6:210.

Chapter 3

All Taken into the One Sacrifice:
The Sacrifice of Christ in the Church of God

By first studying the Scriptures, we have discovered this ever recurrent affirmation: when one is a Christian, one does not live as a self-centered subject. The self has been absorbed into Christ, who gathers his church through his sacrifice. Second, we have read in the works of the main Eastern and Western representatives of the undivided church in the fifth century irrefutable statements showing that the sacrificial quality of the Eucharist is expressed in the sacrificial quality of the community's life and vice versa. For instance, Augustine said to those newly baptized during the Easter Vigil:

"Because he wanted us to be ourselves his sacrifice, which is indicated by where that sacrifice was first put, that is, the sign of the thing that we are; why, then after the consecration is accomplished, we say the Lord's prayer, which you have received and given back."[1]

At the heart of *The City of God*, he explained in a formula already quoted:

"This is the sacrifice of Christians: we, being many, are one body in Christ. And this is also the sacrifice which the church continually celebrates in the sacrament of the altar, known to the faithful, in which the church teaches that it itself is offered in the offering it makes to God."[2]

---

[1] Augustine, *Sermon 227*, in Hill, 4:255.

[2] Augustine, *City of God*, 10.6, in Schaff, 2:183–84, which we have quoted in its entirety in the preceding chapter, pp. 44–45.

The church is the sacrifice which, in Christ, glorifies the Father. Why? Because at the Eucharist, it is transformed into the sacrifice it celebrates. It is in this sense that the Eucharist "makes the church," the church, sacrifice of God.

This very forceful assertion reveals a fundamental insight of the tradition during the first centuries. We saw that Chrysostom reached the same view through another process of thought, underlining its biblical roots. This insight sheds abundant light on the deepest core of the church which God fashions out of faith and the Eucharist.

I. THE SACRIFICE OF MERCY AND SERVICE

1. It is well known that the Letter to the Hebrews insists on the "once for all" *(ephapax)* of the priesthood and sacrifice of Christ (7:27; 9:12, 26; 10:10; see Rom 6:10; 1 Pet 3:18); nevertheless, it ends with a development which brings to mind the solemn text of Matthew 25:31-46:

"Let mutual love [philadelphia] continue. Do not neglect to show hospitality to strangers, for by doing that some have entertained angels without knowing it. Remember those who are in prison, as though you were in prison with them; those who are being tortured, as though you yourselves were being tortured. . . . Do not neglect to do good and to share [koinōnia] what you have, for such sacrifices are pleasing to God" (Heb 13:1-3, 16).

Therefore, in the New Testament, sacrifice is used with a wealth of different meanings. Of course, believers "continually offer a sacrifice of praise to God" (Heb 13:15), thus glorifying God. Then, they bless God by "recalling" God's marvelous deeds of mercy and salvation. But they glorify God also by the sacrifices of mercy through which, in some way, the New Covenant of the Lord's sacrifice bears its full fruit in service to the poor and, more generally, to those who are in the grip of suffering.

We have already met texts from John Chrysostom explicitly linking this Christian conviction with the Eucharist. Let us recall the most powerful:

"This altar is made of Christ's members themselves, and the body of the Lord becomes your altar. Venerate it: you sacrifice the victim on the flesh of the Lord. This altar is more awesome than the one we use here, not just more than the one used in ancient times [in the Old Testament]. No, do not object.

This altar is awesome because of the sacrifice laid upon it; that, the one made of alms, is even more so, not just because of the alms, but because it is the very sacrifice which makes the other awesome. Again, this altar, only stone, becomes holy because Christ's body touches it, but that is holy because it is itself Christ's body. So that altar is more awesome, sisters and brothers, than the one you are standing beside."[3]

What Chrysostom in his oratorical style presents as an opposition, the Christians of the first centuries lived as a seamless whole. The *First Apology* of Justin proves it by showing that very early on (ca. 150), Christian communities associated Eucharist and service to the poor:

"And afterwards we continually remind each other of these things. The wealthy among us help the needy, and we give one another mutual assistance. For everything given us, we bless the Creator of the universe through his Son Jesus Christ and the Holy Spirit. On the day called Sunday, all who live in cities or the country gather together in one place, and we read the memoirs of the apostles or the writings of the prophets for as long as time permits; when the reader has finished, the president instructs us and exhorts us to imitate these good teachings. Then we all rise together and pray. And as we said before, when our prayer is ended, bread, wine, and water are brought; the president likewise offers as best one can prayers and thanksgiving, and the people assent with *Amen. Then there is a distribution to each and a partaking of the bread and wine over which thanks have been given, and the deacons take a portion to the absent. Those who are well to do and are willing give what each thinks fit. What is collected is deposited with the president, who helps the orphans and widows, those who are in want because of sickness or anything else, prisoners, the strangers living among us, in a word, all who are in need."*[4]

---

[3] John Chrysostom, *Homilies on 2 Corinthians* 20, in Schaff, 12:374. On the poor as the altar of God, see *Constitutions of the Holy Apostles* 4.3, in Roberts, 7:433: "But those who receive alms because they are young orphans or old and infirm or sick or raising many children WILL not be blamed; rather, they will be commended. They will be revered as the altar of God and God will honor them because they pray zealously and constantly for those who care for them and because they do not receive indifferently but with their prayers repay to the best of their ability what is given them. These will be blessed by God in eternal life."

[4] Justin, *First Apology*, 67.1–7, in Roberts, 1:185–86.

2. The Eucharist owes this concern for the poor to the human soil in which it is rooted. For in Judaism it was central. Experts say that this concern was made concrete especially by "the plate of the poor," prepared daily, and "the basket of the poor," distributed on the eve of the Sabbath to provide sustenance for the whole week. This service seems to have been preserved in the first Christian community (in Acts 6:1-6, the Hellenist widows complain of being neglected)[5] and was coupled from the first with the eucharistic celebration. The "basket of the poor" probably was delayed to the evening of the Sabbath.[6] This is probably the context which enables us to explain Paul's reaction in 1 Cor 11:17-34.[7]

Because of this, Nicholas Afanassief, an Orthodox theologian, thought that

"in the primitive church, there was no private charitable service, except in a very limited way. Instead, every member brought his or her

[5] Charles Perrot, *Jésus et l'histoire* (Paris: Desclée, 1979) 296–98.

[6] Ibid., 296.

[7] "Such a link between the service of the table and the service of mutual help is reflected in the twofold archetypal account of the Christian meal. The story of the Last Supper is the archetype of the first kind of meal, the group meal; the multiplication of the loaves is the archetype of the second kind, that of the distribution of food. In this case the crowd is in need of food; loaves and fish are collected (see John 6:9), not bought; and the whole thing is multiplied and distributed overabundantly. Is it necessary to add that both stories have in common the anamnesis [remembering] of the same gesture of Jesus, who presides over the meal, blesses, breaks the bread and has it distributed (or distributes it himself) (Mark 6:41; 8:6, 14, 22)? This observation helps us to understand better how in the New Testament, the Greek word *koinōnia* designates both the common table and the service of mutual help; and similarly, how the word *diakonia* designates both the service at table and the collection of money for mutual help. As a consequence, the Christian meal is meant to signify *koinōnia*, communion with the "body of Christ," through the bread distributed, just as the *koinōnia* of the meal of mutual help manifests the community of brothers and sisters through the bread gathered. As St. Paul declares in a sentence which we translate here literally, 'The bread which we break is it not the communion [*koinōnia*] with the body of Christ? For one bread—one body—we, the many, we are, since all of us we share one bread' (1 Cor 10:16-17). The Christian meal is the place par excellence of unity and Christian charity where the Lord continues to distribute what the collection gathers. *The multiplication of the loaves is going on.* A whole program of Christian practice is contained in the account of this miracle, as is the case for the other stories of miracles. *Koinōnia* is built around the same bread distributed, around the same person who continues to distribute it. Here we are touching a fundamental conviction of the early community: it designates the risen One, the ever present Lord, as the one who gathers it and causes it to exist" (ibid., 297–98).

gift of love to the eucharistic assembly. These gifts formed 'the treasury of love' from which one took what was necessary to supply needs. 'If one member suffers, all suffer together with it' (1 Cor 12:26). This suffering of all was relieved by the activity of one person to whom the ministry of charitable service had been entrusted. . . . Such ministry appeared very early in the church; more accurately, it appeared at the same time as the first assembly."[8]

3. The Johannine tradition probably attests to this connection between Eucharist and service of the poor by presenting the washing of the feet at the beginning of a development which seems to prepare readers for reflections on the last meal of Jesus with his disciples (John 13:3-20). It is true that there is no ritual indication of the Eucharist "since there is no mention of bread, wine, eating, or drinking."[9] However, serious exegetes[10] see in this passage a concrete act illustrating the deep meaning of the Eucharist, "communion with Christ and, through it, communion of the disciples among themselves,"[11] cemented by the mutual service that *agapē* implies. "He loved them to the end," "Do you know what I have done to you? . . . If I, your Lord and Teacher, have washed your feet, you also ought to wash one another's feet. For I have set you an example, that you also should do as I have done to you" (John 13:1, 12-15). The act inspired by *agapē*, within which John sets the Last Supper, before the betrayal and the passion (13:1, 2, 12, 21-30), must be found also in the disciples of Christ, designated here as "his own" (*hoi idioi*, 13:1).

[8] Nicholas Afanassief, *L'Église du Saint-Esprit*, Cogitatio fidei 83 (Paris: Cerf, 1975) 234.

[9] Raymond E. Brown, *The Gospel according to John, 13–21*, Anchor Bible 29A (Garden City, N.Y.: Doubleday, 1970) 559. See the short study of E. Schweitzer, "Le Baptême et la Cène dans la littérature johannique," *Les Sacrements d'initiation et les Ministères sacrés, colloque de Tübingen organisé par l'Académie internationale des sciences religieuses* (Paris: Fayard, 1974) 163–78 and the important discussion that follows, in particular the contributions of Rudolf Schnackenburg. See also Francis J. Moloney, "A Sacramental Reading of John 13:1-38," *Catholic Biblical Quarterly* 53 (1991) 237–56.

[10] Thus, after Alfred Firmin Loisy, Maurice Goguel, *L'Eucharistie des origines à Justin Martyr* (Paris: Fischbacher, 1910) 195–96; Oscar Cullmann, *La Foi et le Culte de L'Église primitive* (Neuchâtel: Delachaux and Niestlé, 1963) 196–99; Barnabas Lindars, ed., *The Gospel of John* (Greenwood, S.C.: Attic, 1972) 441–56; Schnackenburg, in *Sacrements d'initiation*.

[11] Cullmann, *Foi et Culte*, 197.

The parallelism with the sentence in Luke's account of the Last Supper is striking, "For who is greater, the one who is at the table or the one who serves? Is it not the one at the table? But I am among you as one who serves" (Luke 22:27). Obviously, this verse carries a demand. It is

"a call to the leaders of the community to assist the poor and needy at the time of the community meal (cf. Acts 6:2). Indeed the leaders must always keep in mind what Jesus had said to the apostles at the multiplication of the loaves in the desert, 'You give them something to eat' (Mark 6:37). When this story was told in the primitive communities, people must have remembered their own community meals: as Jesus had in the past sent the disciples (Mark 6:41; 8:6) to give food to the hungry who had sat down 'in groups' (6:39), so was it done at the community meals. In any case, Paul insists forcefully on the duty of assisting the hungry when he blames the community at Corinth for their lack of regard for the poor (1 Cor 11:20-34). . . .

"Therefore, one must not interpret Luke 22:24-26 in the context of the Last Supper as an invitation to humility; Jesus' words aim at instituting a new order of things: the community leaders must take seriously their duty of serving at table. Therefore, when Jesus orders his apostles to repeat his eucharistic gesture (Luke 22:19), he urges them to join their service to their brothers and sisters at table to the celebration of the Eucharist."[12]

We glimpse here the eschatological dimension of the Eucharist since at the feast of the reign, the Lord will welcome the community at his table (Luke 22:30).

Chapter 13 of John's Gospel—where Judas' betrayal is announced during the meal (13:2, 21-31)—could thus be the place where John evokes the "community's sharing of one table," sealed by the Eucharist, and the necessity of communion that derives from it. Moreover, John would emphasize that this communion is expressed in mutual service.[13] After having hesitated for a long time, we came to the con-

---

[12] Heinz Schürmann, *Le Récit de la dernière Cène* (Le Puy-Lyon, 1965) 71–72. [Der Abendmahlsbericht Lucas 22, 7–38 als Gottesdienstordnung-Gemeindeordnung Lebensordnung (Paderborn: Schoningh, 1963).]

[13] Lindars, *Gospel of John*, 442–44. On the importance which the Church has always given to this ritual, see Brook Foss Westcott, *The Gospel according to St. John*,

clusion that this reading is accurate. And in this case, the text contains an all-important revelation on the nature of the Eucharist. Its institution by the Lord is associated with the will to bring forth communion to the point that the forceful reminder of this will can—for a community which is celebrating the eucharistic meal—sum up the story of the institution. In other words, John suggests the institution by reminding his hearers of its finality, in the context of a meal during which the Lord senses that "the hour to depart from this world and go to the Father" (13:1) is at hand. Thus, it is made clear why the "new commandment" is given following Judas' departure: after the washing of the feet, his conduct had been censured as the sign par excellence of the breaking of communion, "The one who ate my bread has lifted his heel against me" (John 13:18; see also Ps 41):

"Just as I have loved you, you also should love one another. By this everyone will know that you are my disciples, if you have love for one another" (John 13:34-35).

Disciples must make their own Christ's service of "washing the feet," a *diakonia* (service) which belongs with the *leitourgia* (ministry) of the Father's plan.

In this perspective—which to us appears in harmony with John's intention[14]—the Eucharist, where the disciples feed on the Lord "laying down his life" ("placing his soul in the palm of his hand," as Tresmontant translates) effects the osmosis, perceived so well by Augustine, between the "sacrifice" of the Lord and Master and the "sacrifice" of the disciples. The Eucharist is where the two affirmations of John's letter coalesce, "he laid down his life for us—and we ought to lay down our lives for one another" (1 John 3:16). Coming back to the image of John's Gospel, we may say that the Eucharist is the sacrament of the Lord Jesus, the "Father's vine" inseparable from its "branches." These branches bear fruit (15:2, 4, 5, 8, 16), the fruit of the vine which

---

ed. A. Westcott (1908; reprint, Grand Rapids, Mich.: Baker, 1980) 192–93, n. 15 (which refers to the indispensable book by Bingham, 12:4, 10). See also Edwyn Clement Hoskyns, *The Fourth Gospel*, ed. Francis Noël Davey (London: Faber and Faber, 1947) 443–46. Concerning more recent practices, see Peter Jeffrey, "*Mandatum novum do vobis:* Toward a Renewal for the Holy Thursday Footwashing Rite," *Worship* 64 (1990) 107–41.

[14] This is why we modify our position on this point. Lindars' brief but profound remarks in *Gospel of John* have been largely the cause of this change.

glorifies the Father. Now, this fruit reaches full maturity in the act of "laying down one's life" for others (15:13). Therefore, in the Eucharist, one celebrates the sacrifice of the Lord (his "laying down his life") fructifying fully in the "fruit" of the branches that are in him, God's vine, and that in their turn "lay down their lives" for others.

Although this service goes beyond concern for the poor, it obviously includes it. It is possible that John's text alludes to this when recounting what the disciples surmise Jesus said to Judas: "Some thought that, because Judas had the common purse, Jesus was telling him . . . he should give something to the poor" (13:29).

4. The reflections of Chrysostom and many Fathers on the essential link between service to the poor and the sacramental celebration of the body offered in sacrifice have their source here. Paul also speaks of this link as does James when he condemns the lack of welcome shown the poor at the synaxis (Jas 2:1-13). And all this has strong roots in the teaching of the prophets.

"Bringing offerings is futile;
    incense is an abomination to me.
New moon and sabbath and calling of convocation—
    I cannot endure solemn assemblies with iniquity.
Your new moons and your appointed festivals
    my soul hates;
they have become a burden to me,
    I am weary of bearing them.
When you stretch out your hands,
    I will hide my eyes from you;
even though you make many prayers,
    I will not listen;
    your hands are full of blood.
Wash yourselves; make yourselves clean;
    remove the evil of your doings
    from before my eyes;
cease to do evil,
    learn to do good;
seek justice,
    rescue the oppressed,
defend the orphan,
    plead for the widow." (Isa 1:13-17)

And further on:

"Is not this the fast I choose:
   to loose the bonds of injustice,
   to undo the thongs of the yoke,
to let the oppressed go free,
   and to break every yoke?
Is it not to share your bread with the hungry,
   and bring the homeless poor into your house;
when you see the naked, to cover them,
   and not to hide yourself from your own kin?
                . . . .
If you remove the yoke from among you,
   the pointing of the finger, the speaking of evil,
if you offer your food to the hungry
   and satisfy the needs of the afflicted,
then your light shall rise in the darkness
   and your gloom be like the noonday" (Isa 58:6-10).

Much later, the rabbinical tradition was to offer glosses on the relationship between liturgical atonement and works of charity for the little ones. According to it, these works replace the sacrifice of atonement. Quoting the prophet Hosea (6:6), it stresses that God prefers good works above all else. This remark of Rabbi Akiba, who wanted to follow the prophetic tradition, will find place in the Talmud:

"Whoever prolong the time they stay at table prolong their lives; perhaps a poor person will come to whom they will give something to eat. As long as the Temple existed, the altar served to make atonement for the benefit of Israel, but now, the table of private individuals makes atonement for them [by receiving the poor]" (b. Berakhot 55a).

The following anecdote in the *Abot* of Rabbi Nathan confirms this:

"It is told of Rabban Johanan ben Zakkai that he was walking on a road when Rabbi Joshua ran after him and said, 'Woe to us because the house of our life [the Temple], the place where the expiation of our sins took place, has been destroyed.' Johanan answered, 'Do not fear because we have another expiation instead.' Joshua asked, 'And what is it?' Johanan answered, 'It is, "I desire steadfast love and not sacrifice"'" [Hos 6:6].

Another statement by Rabbi Akiba is in the same vein:

"Tineius Rufus asked, 'If your God loves the poor, why does God not take care of them?' Akiba replied, 'It is so that through the poor, we may be delivered from Gehenna'" (b. Baba Batra 10a).

Israel's memory never forgot the book of Tobit: "Almsgiving saves from death and purges away every sin" (12:9). The way to faithfulness to God is attention to the needs of others. The faithfulness of God to God's people responds to this demand. These texts are similar to the patristic texts. Thus:

"Almsgiving is an excellent way to atone for sin. Fasting is better than prayer. Almsgiving is better than both. Charity covers a multitude of sins. The prayer made with a good conscience delivers from death. Happy those who are judged perfect in all this. For almsgiving makes sin less heavy."[15]

The sentence in Hebrews describing "sacrifices [that] are pleasing to God" as good deeds done for the community (13:16) transmits to us the echo of a tradition that has long been part of the consciousness of the people of God and is deeply embedded in it. When the first Christian generations—as early as the days following Pentecost—connect the Eucharist with service to the poor, they thus highlight the essential purpose of the Eucharist for the people, a purpose according to God's will and prepared by God since the covenant with Abraham. The Eucharist is inseparable from what God loves above all: a people which does not accept human misery passively, a people unceasingly engaged in the sacrifice of mutual help and charity, constantly turned toward "others," particularly the most neglected ones whom God prefers.

---

[15] This patristic text is from a homily of the 2nd century, attributed to Clement of Rome, in *Patres Apostolici*, 2 vols., ed. Francis Xavier Funk (Tübingen: Laupp, 1901) 1:298. See Isa 15:22; Amos 5:21-27; Hos 6:6; Mic 6:5-8; Jer 6:20; Zech 7:4-6; Ps 40:7-9; Ps 50:5-15. See *The Fathers according to Rabbi Nathan (Abot of Rabbi Nathan) Version B*, trans. Anthony J. Salardini, Studies in Judaism in Late Antiquity 11 (Leiden: Brill, 1975) 75; Solomon Schechter, *Some Aspects of Rabbinic Theology* (New York: Macmillan, 1909) 296–312; Abraham Cohen, *Le Talmud, exposé synthétique du Talmud et de l'enseignement des Rabbins* (Paris, 1958) 275–84.

II. THE SACRIFICE OF LAYING DOWN ONE'S WHOLE SELF

1. We have noted that in the Gospel of John, the "laying down of one's life" has a larger object than service to the poor. This object is communion. This makes of the church not the unity of a moral person but the center of mutual gift between genuinely alive members of Christ, therefore it makes of the church a sacrifice of *agapē*.

Alluding both to the word of God and the Eucharist (since he quotes 1 Cor 10:16, "the bread that we break, is it not a sharing in the body of Christ?"), Jerome (d. 420) wrote graphically:

"When there is a lack of water and bread in the church, people become a burden to their neighbors, there is discord everywhere, we tear apart the tunic of Christ Jesus whereas the soldiers themselves had not dared to tear it during his passion."[16]

The Eucharist is not just the ecclesial *koinōnia* at the sacramental moment that completes Christian initiation. It keeps and protects it, synaxis after synaxis, maintains the members of Christ within the embrace of the body of reconciliation where the Spirit, which makes them sharers of the Father's life, recreates them.

The Spirit's power of recreation is actualized in the existence of a body which must remain body and not yield to the temptation of breaking apart by letting the gangrene of discord take hold. A broken body is no longer a genuine body. To be able to withstand this temptation, every baptized person receives, in the grace of the broken bread and the shared cup, the power not only to be—*in Christ* the reconciler —but to live *from Christ* the reconciler, as a member through which communion is actualized in the body. The health of the communion, that is, of the ecclesial body of Christ, demands the evangelical health of every member.

It is possible to characterize exactly this "grace of the member" as the grace to overpower the weight of sin present in every believer, in other words the grace to break away from the captivity of "autonomous existence,"[17] "egotistic individualism," "individual survival,"

---

[16] Jerome, *On Ezekiel* 4.216-17, in *PL* 25:50.

[17] This is an expression coined by Christos Yannaras, *La Foi vivante de l'Église, introduction à la théologie orthodoxe* (Paris, 1989) 153 and 157. The same idea is also in Christos Yannaras, *La Liberté de la morale*, Perspective orthodoxe 4 (Geneva, 1982)

life uniquely centered on self. As we have been stressing from the beginning of this book, this does not mean simply that the life of the members of Christ's body is no longer guided exclusively by individual duties. Because they are saved "in Christ," baptized in the one Spirit, and nourished with the one bread, Christians are in essence *beings-who-are-with,* not individuals but persons-in-communion. For them, indeed, the necessary relationship *with* others no longer depends on a command or mandate. It is the very definition of being a Christian. The Eucharist rescues the person from the fundamental corruption which is the rupture of the relationship with God and with others in the suffocating imprisonment within oneself. The Eucharist roots the person in the *koinōnia* of the body of Christ. This *koinōnia,* to say it once more, fundamentally consists in the gathering of the multitude by the one body of the Lord in the act of reconciliation through self-emptying. What is here is not an addition of individual lives: the *koinōnia* is communion in a new mode of existence, defined by the paschal sacrifice of the Lord "giving himself" to the Father and *to* others.

2. Tradition will find in John's Gospel the radical demand following from this letting-go of self. The traditional formula, "the grace of the Eucharist is *agapē*" must be interpreted within this perspective, not in the psychologizing and utterly private perspective which is the constant temptation of the West. We have seen in Chrysostom bold statements on the gift of *agapē* which the Eucharist is and the obligation of love that results from it. These statements agree with the letting-go of self:

"We glorify him . . . not only for pouring out [his blood] but for giving it to all of us. 'So if you want blood,' he says, 'do not cover the altar of idols with the blood of beasts, but cover my altar with my blood.' Tell me, what can be more tremendous than this? What can be more tenderly kind? This is what lovers do. *When they see those whom they love longing for what belongs to strangers and despising their own, they give what is theirs and so persuade them to turn from the gifts of others. However,*

43–56, 79–95. One will notice similar views in John D. Zizioulas' numerous studies on the subject, collected in *Being as Communion: Studies in Personhood and the Church,* Contemporary Greek Theologians 4 (Crestwood, N.Y., St. Vladimir's Seminary, 1985).

lovers display this liberality in goods and money and garments, but in blood, never. Whereas Christ, even in this, has shown his care and fervent love for us. . . . *Now if we are all nourished by the same thing and all become the same thing, why do we not all exhibit the same love, and in this also become one?"*[18]

Through the channel of Thomas Aquinas, this same thought has become the official doctrine of the West: "The Eucharist is termed the sacrament of charity, which is the bond of perfection [Col 3:14],"[19] "This sacrament confers grace spiritually *[spiritualiter]* together with the virtue of charity. . . . Hence it is that the soul is spiritually nourished through the power of this sacrament by being spiritually gladdened and, as it were, inebriated with the sweetness of the Divine goodness, according to Song of Songs 5:1: 'Eat, friends, drink,/ and be drunk with love.'"[20] And the office of the feast of *Corpus Christi* (the Body and Blood of Christ)[21] is like a concerto built around this theme, never explicit but always perceptible. There is no doubt about it: both East and West see in the Eucharist the sacrament of love, love received, love that must spread abroad.

But what do we mean by love? A few lines from an Anglican theologian seem to us a perfect description of *agapē* at its finest, the very subject of our reflection:

"This is because love, in its ontological sense, is letting-be. Love usually gets defined in terms of union, or the drive toward union, but such a definition is too egocentric. Love does indeed lead to community, but to aim primarily at uniting the other person to oneself, or oneself to him, is not the secret of love and may even be destructive of genuine community. Love is letting-be, not of course in the sense of standing off from someone or something, but in the positive and active sense of enabling-to-be. When we talk of 'letting-be,' we are to understand both parts of this hyphenated expression in a strong sense—'letting' as 'empowering,' and 'be' as enjoying the maximal range of being that is open to the particular being concerned. Most

[18] John Chrysostom, *Homilies on 1 Corinthians*, 24.3-4, in Schaff, 11:139, 140.
[19] *ST IIIa*, q73, a3, ad 3 (p. 236).
[20] Ibid., q79, a1, ad 2 (p. 352).
[21] See P. M. Gy, "L'Office du 'Corpus Christi' et saint Thomas d'Aquin," *RSTP* 64 (1980) 491–507.

typically, 'letting-be' means helping a person into the full realization of his potentialities for being; and the greatest love will be costly, since it will be accomplished by the spending of one's own being.

"Love is letting-be even where this may demand the loosening of the bonds that bind the beloved person to oneself; this might well be the most costly of demands, and it is in the light of this kind of love that a drive toward union may seem egocentric. The parent, for instance, really loves the child by letting the child come into his potentialities for independent living, not by keeping him close."[22]

The Eucharist is sacrament of *agapē* because it gives to those who really feed on the body of Christ the power of the Spirit to accomplish, according to each one's means, toward the members of the ecclesial body what the Johannine literature and Paul regard as the core of Christ Jesus' work: "I lay down my life for the sheep" (John 10:15); "[he] loved me and gave himself for me" (Gal 2:20). The sacramental body and blood transmit the gift which Christ made in the act of delivering himself up. And did he not deliver himself up precisely to enable humankind to be what God the Father wants it to be? Abiding in him, the disciples are called to actively represent in the world what was the core of his life and mission, through a love which is not sentimental but concrete.[23] At the resurrection, "*Jesus himself* became *the charisma of God*,"[24] that is, the bearer of the Spirit's power associated

---

[22] John Macquarrie, *Principles of Christian Theology*, 2nd ed. (New York: Scribner's, 1977) 348–49. This text was brought to mind by Jerome Murphy O'Connor, *L'Existence chrétienne selon saint Paul*, Lectio divina 80 (Paris: Cerf, 1974); however, he cites this text only partially and according to the first edition of the book. We cite according to the second edition.

[23] See Claude Tresmontant, *Évangile de Jean* (Paris, 1984) 402. James Leslie Houlden, *A Commentary on the Johannine Epistles* (New York: Harper and Row, 1973) 99–100, rightly says about the term *agapē*, "It is defined by Christ's dying *for us*. His action shows the very meaning of the word. Moreover, it shows what the duty to love entails for his followers: they too must give their lives, not for others in general, but as we should expect (cf. 1 John 3:11; John 13:34), for each other."

[24] James D. G. Dunn, *Jesus and the Spirit* (Philadelphia: Westminster, 1975) 325. The author has this striking expression, "In Paul then *the distinctive mark of the Spirit becomes his Christness*" (ibid.; Dunn's emphasis). The link between the risen *Kurios* (Lord) and the Spirit is essential to the understanding of the deep meaning of the sacraments. On the one hand, the Lord vivifies only by "giving us a share in his Spirit." On the other hand, only in the Spirit can the believing community stand before the Father "in Christ." The Orthodox tradition rightly remarks on the poverty of the Western theologies on this point.

with the very act of the new creation in his paschal sacrifice. Those who feed on the body at the eucharistic table are taken up into this charism of God, charism of *agapē,* in order to "recreate," "give life," "let-be." But it is a letting-go of self which corresponds precisely to what, as we have seen, is the authentic place of the branch in the vine, the member in the body. The eucharistic bread is what makes Peter and Mary able to live *before God,* not as the individuals Peter and Mary, but as Peter member of the body of Christ, and Mary member of the body of Christ, filled with a life that goes beyond them and is no longer merely "for them." Is this not also the meaning of Romans 6:11? "The death he died, he died to sin, once for all; but the life he lives, he lives to God. So you also must consider yourselves dead to sin and alive to God in Christ Jesus *[en Christō Iēsou]."* Thus, we find again the deeply sacrificial quality of the Eucharist; it is a sacrament *of the* gift, which makes *a* gift of the believers themselves.

III. THE SACRIFICE OF LIFE IN THE PRIESTLY PEOPLE

1. The relation of sacrifice to the whole of ecclesial life is all-encompassing. For when used by Christians, the term sacrifice has in the New Testament a very wide application: it includes all the evangelical actions which make up the fabric of an entire life. This is the meaning of affirmations like, "[You are] built into a spiritual house . . . to offer spiritual sacrifices acceptable to God through Jesus Christ" (1 Pet 2:5); "I appeal to you . . . by the mercies of God, to present your bodies as a living *sacrifice,* holy and acceptable to God, which is your *spiritual worship"* (Rom 12:1; see 15:14-21); "[my blood] poured out as a sacrifice offered as a *libation over the sacrifice* and the offering *[leitourgia]* of your faith" (Phil 2:17); "I have received from Epaphroditus the gifts you sent, a fragrant offering, a *sacrifice* acceptable and pleasing to God" (Phil 4:18). It is no longer just a question of the help given to the little ones and the poor—as in the Letter to the Hebrews—which is an important element of the "sacrificial" activity but is not the whole of it. It is no longer just a question of ritual liturgy. It is a question of life *as such,* empowered by the process of its being laid down.

Already Philo (d. ca. 50) had shown several times that in the spirit of the Old Covenant, faithful believers offer their own virtues to God, in which they recognize above all a gift from God. Therefore virtues—especially faith, are God's most valuable gift—the "unsullied victims" of the "spiritual sacrifice" which is one's own life. By totally surrendering themselves to God, faithful believers become a holocaust: "For the virtues are perfect and blameless offerings, and so are actions in accord with virtue";[25] "the altar is full of spotless victims, I mean, of innocent and completely purified souls."[26] Judaism specifies[27] that on God's altar,[28] sincere believers "offer [their] soul[s]," as an offering based on their determination to be faithful to God's will, even to the point of sacrificing their lives if the circumstances warrant it. This determination comes from faith which for this reason is, according to Philo, "a faultless, the finest offering . . . on festivals which are not the feasts of mortals."[29] Those, then, are a "whole burnt offering" who by their lives

"have been duly consecrated by their zeal, fervent and fiery, consuming the flesh, easily and vehemently directed towards godliness, a zeal

---

[25] Philo, *On Flight and Finding* 18, in Philo, *Works,* 322. See Philo, *On the Birth of Abel and the Sacrifices Offered by Him and His Brother Cain* 51, in ibid., 100: "the virtues, faultless and most worthy offerings, and abominated by the fool," such is the sacrifice to God.

[26] Philo, *Flight and Finding* 80, in Philo, *Works,* 328.

[27] See the interesting complementary note 11 in Philo, *De Fuga et inventione* [On Flight and Finding], ed. Esther Starobinski-Safran, Les Œuvres de Philon d'Alexandrie 17 (Paris: Cerf, 1970) 275: "The idea that God accepts sacrifices only if they are accompanied by pure intention is strongly emphasized by the prophets themselves, faithful to the Pentateuch (See Lev 1:3, commented upon in b. ʿArakhin 21a), notably in the famous passage from Isaiah 1:11-16 (See 1 Sam 15:22; Amos 5:21-24; Mic 6:7-8; Jer 6:20; 7:21-23; see also Ps 59:12 and especially Ps 51:19, commented upon in b. Sanhedrin 13b). Similar affirmations are found also in the Hellenistic Jewish literature, as *Aristeas* 11.234 shows. See on this subject Harry Austryn Wolfson, *Philo,* 2 vols. (Cambridge: Harvard, 1947) 2:242ff. The rabbinical literature has abundant texts in the same vein (see b. Shevuʿot 15a; b. Zevaḥim 7b; b. Berakhot 23a). Philo interprets the sacrifice and rites in the allegorical manner. See Isaak Heinemann, *Philons griechische und judische Bildung,* 2nd ed. (Hildesheim: Olms, 1973) 66. It is the soul itself, in all its purity, that the wise person offers to God (*Allegorical Interpretation* 3.141, to be compared with the image of the soul offered in sacrifice, as presented in b. Menaḥot 104b. From there, one can deduce the concept, fundamental in Judaism, of the *messirout nephesh,* literally "the offering of the soul," which exhorts Jews to fulfill God's commands with complete self-denial and to be ready to sacrifice their lives in order to proclaim their faithfulness to God. See Rashi, *On Leviticus* 2.1, and Seforno, *On Leviticus* 1:2). For Philo, the altar is the symbol of the total forgiveness of sins (*Special Laws* 1.215); therefore, the altar remains inaccessible to those who have not truly purified themselves."

[28] Which Chrysostom and the *Apostolic Constitutions* will identify especially with the poor, thus making the actions accomplished for their benefit the "sacrifice" par excellence.

[29] Philo, *On the Cherubim* 2.85, in Philo, *Works,* 89.

not belonging to this world but akin to God. And not going up to the altar by the customary steps, for the Law prohibits that, but pressing rapidly onwards with a favorable wind and conducted up to the very threshold of heaven, they dissolve into ethereal beams like a whole burnt offering.[30]

"The wise consecrate their entire soul, worthy to be offered to God because it is free from impurity, intentional or unintentional,[31]

"[because] one should not bring to the altar of God, by which the remission and complete pardon of all sins and transgressions is obtained . . . what is wandering on the trackless road of injustice and impiety, having turned out of the way which leads to virtue and moral excellence; for it would be folly to suppose that sacrifices do not obtain pardon for offenses, but act as a reminder of them."[32]

2. Here one senses the close kinship with Paul's exhortation to the Romans, "I appeal to you *therefore* . . . to present your bodies *[ta sōmata]* as a living sacrifice *[thusia],* holy and acceptable to God, which is your spiritual worship *[latreia]*" (Rom 12:1).[33] It is obvious that in this verse, punctuated by liturgical terms, Paul considers concrete life (the life that takes place in the *sōmata*) the object of the sacrifice pleasing to God:

[30] Philo, *On Dreams* 2.67, in ibid., 392.

[31] Philo, *Allegorical Interpretation* 3.141, in ibid., 66.

[32] Philo, *Special Laws* 1.215, in ibid., 554. For a synthetic view of Philo's thought in this domain, see particularly Jean Laporte, *La Doctrine eucharistique chez Philon D'Alexandrie,* Théologie historique 16 (Paris: Beauchesne, 1972) 127–40; Annie Jaubert, *La Notion d'Alliance dans le judaïsme aux abords de l'ère chrétienne,* Patristica Sorboniensia 6 (Paris: Seuil, 1963) 168–70; 399–400. The study of Valentin Nikiprowetzky, "La Spiritualisation des sacrifices et le Culte sacrificiel au Temple de Jérusalem chez Philon d'Alexandrie," *Semitica* (Cahiers publiés par l'Institut d' études sémitiques de l'université de Paris) 17 (1967) 97–116, seems to us particularly important for bringing nuances into overly hasty and sweeping affirmations. We shall come back to this point.

[33] See the very fine discussion by Heinrich Schlier, "L'essence de l'exhortation apostolique d'après l'Épître aux Romains 12:1-21," in *Le Temps de l'Église* [Die Zeit der Kirche], trans. Françoise Corin, Cahiers de l'actualité religieuse 14 (Tournai: Casterman, 1961) 85–99; also Ernst Käsemann, *Commentary on Romans,* trans. and ed. Geoffrey W. Bromiley (Grand Rapids, Mich.: Eerdmans, 1980) 325–31; Charles Harold Dodd, *The Epistle of Paul to the Romans* (London: Collins, 1959) 189–93; William Hendriksen *Exposition of Paul's Epistle to the Romans,* 2 vols. (Grand Rapids, Mich.: Baker, 1981) 401–7; Raymond Corriveau, *The Liturgy of Life: A Study of the Ethical Thought of St. Paul in His Letters to the Early Christian Communities,* Studia 25 (Brussels: Desclée de Brouwer, 1970) especially 155–85.

"The mercy of God demands our life. And it demands that we retain nothing whatsoever of it, but that we place it at the disposal of God, withholding nothing. It demands that our life be a sacrifice that we always keep in front of our eyes, without shutting it up in our inner being. All this is understood in the notion of *parastēsai* (presenting) on which, in the context, the accent is placed rather strongly. The moment of the sacrifice is forcefully emphasized by the fact that we must offer our "bodies." Of course, *ta sōmata*, like *ta melē* in Rom 6:13, means ourselves. But the term *ta sōmata* is used intentionally. It is a reminder of the gift of total and real life, whose form of existence is our body. The mercy of God exhorts us to the sacrifice of our real existence."[34]

This sacrifice must not be confused with a ritual act accomplished at sacred times, in sacred places, in conformity with sacred laws. It is identical with life in its daily unfolding.[35] As a response to God's mercy—"I appeal to you *therefore (oun)*"—the sacrifice of an animal or a merely ritual liturgy are insufficient. The only adequate offering is that of life itself led in faithfulness to the divine will;[36] that is the offering of what is most precious and all-encompassing in a person, her or his life as a "saved" person indwelt by the Spirit of God. Such is true "spiritual" worship *(logikē latreia)*, which is in accord with the essential nature of things.[37]

This understanding of sacrifice, which Augustine was to preserve (in the text from *The City of God*, 10.6, quoted above), is present throughout the early tradition. It is found in Clement of Rome[38], in the *Didache*,[39] probably in the Shepherd of Hermas as well.[40] Peter Chryso-

---

[34] Schlier, *Temps de l'Église*, 92–93; he sheds light on this text by referring to Rom 6:13; 8:13; 15:2; 1 Cor 6:11; 2 Cor 4:10-11; 8:9; Phil 2:17; Eph 5:12.

[35] This is well emphasized in Käsemann, *Romans*, 329.

[36] As is well shown by Hendriksen, *New Testament Commentary*, 403.

[37] On the meaning of *logikos*, see Käsemann, *Romans*, 328–29; Charles Kingsley Barrett, *A Commentary on the Epistle to the Romans*, Harper's New Testament Commentaries (New York: Harper, 1971) 231.

[38] 1 Cor 18:17; 35:12; 52:3-4 (which quotes Ps 50:3-19; Ps 49:16-23).

[39] *Didache* 14.1-3. See the article of B. Grimonprez-Damm, "Le Sacrifice eucharistique dans la *Didachè*," *Revue des Sciences religieuses* 64 (1990) 9–25. Is the author right in seeing in the use of *thusia* (sacrifice) in this passage only the mutual help and good works which we have shown to be linked with the eucharistic celebration? For our part, we would be much more cautious. But he is right in stressing the communal character of this *thusia* and its kinship with Rom 12:1.

[40] Shepherd of Hermas 56.8, in Apostolic Fathers, trans. Francis x. Glimm et al. (New York: Cima [1947]). See also Ptolemy, *Letter to Flora* 5.10, in Ptolemy, *Lettre à*

logus (d. 450), bishop of Ravenna, was to give it its strongest and most explicit expression, particularly in his sermons 108 and 109:

"Let us now listen to the Apostle's exhortation. 'I exhort you to present your bodies.' This request has raised all to the priestly rank. 'To present your bodies as a living sacrifice.' O unheard of purpose of the Christian priesthood. Because human beings are both victim and priest for themselves! Because they need not to go beyond themselves to find what they are to immolate to God! Because they, with themselves and in themselves and for themselves bring their offering to God! Because they remain the victim and at the same time do not cease to be the priest! Because the victim is immolated and still lives! Because the priest who will make atonement is unable to die! Wonderful indeed is this sacrifice where the body is offered without [the slaying of] a body, and the blood without bloodshed. . . .

"That is what the Prophet sang: 'Sacrifices and offerings you have not desired / but a body you have prepared for me' [Ps 40:6, LXX, quoted in Heb 10:5]. Be, O people, be both a sacrifice to God and God's priest. Do not forget what the divine authority has entrusted to you. Put on the robe of holiness, gird yourselves with the belt of chastity. Let Christ be the covering of your heads. Let the cross remain on your foreheads. Inscribe on your breasts the sign of divine wisdom. Always keep the incense of prayer burning as your perfume. Take up the sword of the Spirit. Place your hearts on the altar. And thus prepare your bodies as a sacrifice, full of confidence in God.

"God looks for faith, not death; thirsts for self-dedication, not blood; is propitiated by fervor, not by killing. God gave proof of this when God asked holy Abraham to sacrifice his son. What besides his own body was Abraham immolating in his child? What besides faith was God looking for in the father, since God ordered the son to be offered but did not allow him to be killed?

"O people, strengthened by such an example, offer your bodies. Do not just slay them; cut them up into all their members, that is, the virtues. For, the evils of sin within you die as often as you offer the entrails of your virtues to God. Offer up your faith so that your faithlessness may be punished. Immolate your fasts so that your gluttony may

Flora, 2nd ed., trans. Gilles Quispel, SC 24bis (1966): "Thus, the Savior ordered us to make sacrifices, not by offering animals devoid of reason or by offering perfumes, but by praise, glorification, spiritual thanksgiving, charity, and service for the good of others."

cease. Sacrifice your chastity so that your lust may die. Put on your piety so that your impiety may be put off. Invite your mercy so that your avarice may be evicted. And you should always offer up your holiness as a sacrifice so that your stupidity may be consumed.

"Thus your bodies will become your victim, if it has not been wounded by the traits of your sins. Your bodies live, O people, they live every time you offer to God your living virtues so that your vices may die. Those who deserve to be slain by the life-giving sword cannot die. May our God, who is the way, the truth, and the life, deliver us from death and lead us to life."

This passage from *Sermon 108* is made explicit in *Sermon 109:*

"'To present your bodies as a sacrifice, living, holy, pleasing to God.' Human beings please not by the fact that they live, but that they live justly. They become sacrificial victims not just by offering themselves to God, but by offering themselves to God in a holy way. A blemished victim angers God just as an unblemished victim propitiates God. Listen to God: 'Do not offer to me anything lame, or half-blind, or polluted because it is intended for death, but something mature without blemish' [see Lev 22:20]. And so it is that the Apostle seeks a living sacrifice for God. . . .

"Cain is proof of this. Ungrateful priest, he shared with God, from whom he had received everything, the poorest offerings and burnt the worst part of them on the altar while keeping the best part for himself. And so he gave offense. The upshot was that in this evil sharing with his Maker, he separated himself and his descendants from both life and the human race.

"And so, let us follow Abel to his reward, not accompany Cain to his punishment. Abel brought a lamb to God's altar; he was accepted as a lamb. Cain brought hay; he made his own torch which set him afire."[41]

But Cyprian had already contributed an ecclesiological touch to this view which is dear to him. Common life itself is a sacrifice to God:

[41] Peter Chrysologus *Sermon 108*, in *PL* 52:500–1; *Sermon 109*, in *PL* 52:501–3; [also in *Saint Peter Chrysologus, Selected Sermons*, trans. George E. Ganss, The Fathers of the Church (New York: Father of the Church, Inc., 1953) 168–70, 172–73]. The complete text of these two sermons would be worth quoting.

"Our peace and mutual harmony, this is the greatest sacrifice to God—and a people united into one in the unity of the Father and the Son and the Holy Spirit."[42]

This important quotation has a definite ecclesial implication into which we must now go more deeply.

3. The thought of Philo accords with the New Testament text which has become in the West the classic reference on this question: "Let yourselves be built into a spiritual house, to be a *hierateuna hagion* [holy priestly community], *to offer spiritual sacrifices acceptable to God through Jesus Christ*" (1 Pet 2:5); "you are a *basileion hierateuma* [priestly dwelling of the king], the *ethnos hagion* (holy nation)" (2:9).[43] We have already met with these phrases.

To characterize the ecclesial community, 1 Peter repeats an affirmation from Exodus 19:5-6—"you shall be for me a priestly kingdom and a holy nation"—as Jewish tradition read it by applying the word "priests" to the whole nation. Besides, the Greek Septuagint had transformed the plural "priests" into a singular, *hierateuma,* unknown in secular language. It thus underlined the corporate aspect of this common priesthood. In its translation of Exod 23:22, the Septuagint added a sentence to the original text: God promises to make the people God's *basileion* (royal dwelling) and God's *hierateuma* (God's priestly body) as well as God's holy nation. It was a priesthood promised to the people *as such,* a manner of being and a quality of the people of God *as such,* a mission belonging to their identity as God's people. *As body,* it was called, in its solidarity, to a "priestly" function of "service to the glory of the living God" among the nations. The author of 1 Peter sees in the ecclesial community, composed of both Jews and pagans, the fulfillment *(teleiōsis)* of this promise. It is, *as a community,* this priestly body of the living God. Its priesthood does not come from a collection of the priesthoods of all its faithful, as if it were made up of a sum

[42] Cyprian, *On the Lord's Prayer* 23, in Roberts, 8:414. This peace, this community make it impossible for anyone to pray only for himself or herself; see also ibid. 8.4-5.

[43] We have often studied this text, see in particular Jean-Marie-Roger Tillard, "Sacerdoce," in *DSp* 91 (1988) 7–10 (where we give a rather extensive bibliography); Tillard, "La Qualité sacerdotale du ministère," *NRT* 95 (1973) 481–514. See also John Hall Elliott, *The Elect and the Holy: An Exegetical Examination of 1 Peter 2:4-10 and the Phrase* βασίλειον ἱεράτευμα (Leiden: Brill, 1966); Pierre Grelot, "Le Sacerdoce commun des fidèles dans le Nouveau Testament," *Esprit et Vie* 94 (1984) 138–44.

priests. The community of believers *as such*, the organic totality that it is, is *as such* priestly.

Specialists agree that the "spiritual sacrifices" which this "priestly community" offers are—in accord with Philo's thought and with Rom 12:1 and Heb 13:16—the actions, the decisions, the typical ways of leading a human life which faith motivates. These are inspired by the example of Christ (1 Pet 2:21) and made fruitful by the Spirit (1 Pet 4:14). In a word, they are the actions of baptismal life, among which, as the author stresses, those that inspire the relationship with *others* (Christians and even non-Christians) hold a place of honor. However, in this *hierateuma hagion*, the members cannot act by cutting themselves off from the community *as such*. It is to it *as such* that the sacrifice of Christ and the Spirit have been given. The only way to participate in it is to enter into this common gift.

Moreover, the reason believers live a Christian life is not just for their own salvation. It also involves the faithfulness of the community *as such* to its collective vocation. For just as an individual member of the community does not bring to it a "priesthood" which would enhance that of the others—since, enrolled through baptism in the *hierateuma hagion*, each member shares in the "priesthood" which *as such* the community possesses—so each member, by his or her personal conduct, has a part in the mission of witness to salvation, which is the mission of the community *as such*. Personal acts are *in* the spiritual sacrifice of "the chosen race, the priestly house of the king, the holy nation, God's own people" so that those who were not God's people, having now become God's people, and those who had not received mercy, having now received mercy, "may proclaim God's mighty acts" (1 Pet 2:9-10).

A race, a nation are something more than the sum of the individuals they include. They are more than the result of the increase in the wealth that their members supply. Their specific qualities transcend the accumulation of individual gifts. In fact, on many levels, the former precede and condition the latter. For instance, these specific qualities confer a character (even a physical character), a cast of mind, a way of thinking, a heredity, a human rootedness which make an African act and think in a certain way, and a German in another way.[44]

[44] Ernest Renan, "La Réforme intellectuelle et morale de la France," in *La Réforme intellectuelle et morale* (Paris: Calmann-Levy, 1871) 47–48, wrote, "A country is not the mere addition of the individuals that it comprises, but a soul, a conscience, a person, a living resultant."

Analogically, this holds also for the church, "race," "nation," "people" of God. It is the church which gives to the priesthood of its members its particular color, to their spiritual sacrifices their finality.

That all this is not pure personal interpretation, that the great tradition has thought likewise, we discover in several patristic texts. Certainly, the most explicit is a passage from the *Liber de Promissionibus* generally attributed to Quodvultdeus (d. ca. 453):

"This same Solomon built for the Lord this magnificent Temple, made with marvelous splendor, dedicated with all his royal power [see 1 Kgs 6–8]. His father had desired to build this temple but had not been permitted to realize it [see 2 Sam 7:5] because he had struck down many peoples in his military campaigns and was told that having shed blood in abundance on the earth, he could not build a house for God, a task that would fall to his son, a man of peace [see 1 Chr 22:8-9]. But this edifice announces the spiritual temple, for it is written that the Almighty does not dwell in shrines made by human hands [see Acts 17:24]. *This is why our King, the true peace, Christ the Lord, building with living stones a spiritual house, that is, the hearts of his faithful* [see 1 Pet 2:5], *not only built a temple in each faithful person but also built a single temple out of all the faithful.* To these faithful, Paul says, 'Do you not know that you are God's temple and that God's Spirit dwells in you?' [1 Cor 3:16]. *Inside this temple, spiritual victims are offered to God by the One who is also the high priest* [see 1 Pet 2:5]. 'For he is our peace; in his flesh he has made both groups into one'" [Eph 2:14].[45]

Chrysostom gives us proof that the East shares the same view:

"There are occasions when there is no difference at all between the priest and those under him, for instance, when we participate in the awesome mysteries. For all of us alike are counted worthy of the same things, not as it was under the old Law where the priest ate one thing and those under him another and it was unlawful for the people to eat what the priest ate. But it is not like that now: one body and one cup is set before all. And it is the same in the prayers; there one can see that the people contribute much, and both the priest and the people pray

---

[45] Quodvultdeus, *Liber de Promissionibus* 2.27.58, in *Livre des promesses et des prédictions de Dieu*, trans. René Braun, SC 101–2 (1964) 2:431. See also Ambrose, *On the Mysteries* 29, in St. Ambrose, *On the Sacraments and On the Mysteries*, trans. T. Thompson, ed. J. H. Srawley (London: S.P.C.K., 1950) 133.

together for the possessed and those doing penance. All say one prayer, a prayer overflowing with pity. . . . Again, in the awesome mysteries themselves, the priest prays for the people and the people pray for the priest. . . . The prayer of thanksgiving is also prayed in common; the priest does not give thanks alone, but with all the people. The priest begins, next they assent that it is 'meet and right so to do,' then the priest begins the thanksgiving. . . . Now, I have said all this so that each one of you, the laity, will be aware, will understand that we are all one body and that the differences between us are like the differences between our bodies' members. We should not throw everything on the priests but care for the whole church as our common body. . . . For we should all live in the church as in a single house; we should all behave towards one another as if we were one body, just as there is one Baptism, one table, one fountain, one creation, and also one Father."[46]

4. In Romans (15:14-21), Paul presents his apostolate in a sacrificial perspective: he desires to make the pagans a *prosphora,* an offering to God. First Peter adds a new note. According to it, the Christians' missionary activity pertains to the priesthood of the people of God *as such.* It ends its description of the nature of the "holy priestly community" with the phrase "God's own people in order that you may proclaim the mighty acts [of God]" (1 Pet 2:9). It continues, "Conduct yourselves honorably among the Gentiles so that . . . they may see your honorable deeds and glorify God when he comes to judge" (1 Pet 2:12). The goal of the witness, which shortly afterward, tradition was to call mission, is not only expansion, the covering of vast territories, everywhere. It is primarily the glorification of God by the realization of God's eternal plan which is not limited to garnering the greatest possible number of "the saved." For it also implies that creation is "completed" and in particular that humankind may truly become "the-humankind-that-God-wants." In other words, the goal of the mission is at once quantitative (the whole of humanity) and qualitative (the humanity which God wants and which glorifies God). The newness brought about by the gospel is not a newness arising out of nothing, the appearance of a *neon* (something new), of a totally novel thing. Because we are speaking of the newness of salvation, this newness presupposes the preser-

[46] Chrysostom, *Homilies on 2 Corinthians* 18, in Schaff, 12:365–66. Compare with Leo the Great, *Homily for the Anniversary of His Episcopal Ordination* 4.1, in *PL* 54:148–49.

vation of a reality to be made fruitful by the grace of the Spirit. It is a *kainon* (a newness) of renewal, in which creative design and redemptive plan blend in order that God may triumph.

Therefore, missionary commitment also has a sacrificial character, for the glory of the living God. It is an integral part of the "spiritual sacrifices" of the priestly community *as such*. It is worship more than proselytism. This explains why proclamation of the word, so strongly emphasized by Paul (Rom 10:14-21), and witness *(martyria)* call for one another. This witness is not limited to generosity and the particular charisms of certain members whose life challenges "those outside." It pertains to the "holy priestly community built . . . to offer spiritual sacrifices acceptable to God through Jesus Christ." In brief, it pertains to the priesthood of the church and its sacrifice.

IV. THE SACRIFICE CELEBRATED, UNIFIED, AND NOURISHED BY THE EUCHARIST

1. Since "spiritual sacrifice" is for every believer the way to actualize the gospel in union with the priestly body in its entirety, one understands the deep bond between Eucharist and spiritual sacrifice, highlighted in patristic texts. At the eucharistic synaxis the Spirit, through the dynamism of the unique sacrifice of Christ, gathers, in the unity of the body of Christ—inseparable from its head whose sacrament is celebrated here and now—the "spiritual sacrifice" of the "priestly community."

Because of the scattering of individuals and their lives through time and space, the "spiritual sacrifice" is lived in small fractions in the daily and historical life of the ecclesial body. As Augustine said when speaking of communion with the passion of Christ in a text already quoted:

"The body of Christ groans in affliction until the end of the world, when all afflictions will pass away, and this human being groans and calls upon God, and each of us, our own way, has her or his part in that cry of the whole body. You have cried during the days of your life, and your days have passed away. Another has come after you, and cried in her days. You here, she there, another elsewhere: the body of Christ cries all the day, its members departing and succeeding one another. Only one human being endures to the end of the world, and it is the members of Christ who cry."[47]

[47] *Exp on Ps* 86 [85].5, in Schaff, 8:411.

However, this unique and indivisible Christ, "in a state of sacrifice," offering one unique and indivisible "spiritual sacrifice" in the diversity of his members (joined to their life-giving head) is extended into space and place, distended in the time of history and eternity. But at the eucharistic synaxis, its totality is sacramentally gathered and celebrated. Not only are Christians of the same region assembled *epi to auto* (in one place) with their diversity of social status and sometimes race and language, but they also celebrate the sacrament in communion with the saints in heaven, even with all those who will gather at the Lord's table until the parousia. The East speaks of this presence of the glorious church by its icons and the mention of the saints in the epiclesis. We quote the one from the liturgy of John Chrysostom:

"We also offer you this spiritual worship for the fathers, patriarchs, prophets, apostles, preachers, evangelists, martyrs, confessors, virgins, and ascetics who in faith have entered their rest, and for every just person well grounded in faith, above all our Lady, the Mother of God, the always Virgin Mary, Saint John the Forerunner and Baptizer, the holy apostles worthy of every praise, Saint N., whose memory we are celebrating, and all the saints, through whose prayers we ask you to protect us. Remember also all those who fell asleep in the hope of resurrection to eternal life and grant them rest in the place where the light of your face shines."[48]

In the West, the Roman Canon (Eucharistic Prayer 1) is as explicit as one could wish. Thus at Easter,

"In union with the whole Church we celebrate that day when Jesus Christ, our Lord, rose from the dead in his human body. We honor Mary, the ever-virgin mother of Jesus Christ our Lord and God. We honor Joseph, her husband, the apostles and martyrs Peter and Paul, Andrew, James, John, Thomas, James, Philip, Bartholomew, Matthew, Simon and Jude; we honor Linus, Cletus, Clement, Sixtus, Cornelius, Cyprian, Lawrence, Chrysogonus, John and Paul, Cosmas and Damian and all the saints. . . .

"For ourselves, too, we ask some share in the fellowship of your apostles and martyrs, with John the Baptist, Stephen, Matthias,

---

[48] Anaphora of John Chrysostom, in Enzo Lodi, *Enchiridion Euchologicum Fontium Liturgicorum* (Rome: Edizioni Liturgiche, 1979), nos. 2896–2901, 1271–81.

Barnabas, Ignatius, Alexander, Marcellinus, Peter, Felicity, Perpetua, Agatha, Lucy, Agnes, Cecilia, Anastasia and all the saints. Though we are sinners, we trust in your mercy and love. Do not consider what we truly deserve, but grant us your forgiveness."

If every Christian is "a living and spiritual stone of the holy temple where God dwells,"[49] then the Eucharist is the ecclesial moment when the "spiritual sacrifice" of the whole temple finds its true expression in communion. It is as though each one and all together flow into the source of the sacrifice of holy life, the paschal sacrifice of Christ made present. The synaxis is the sacramental celebration in which the sacrifice of the church flows into Christ. Let us quote again the few lines from Augustine which say this in a marvelous way:

"The whole redeemed city, that is, the assembly or community of the saints, is offered to God as our sacrifice through the great high priest who, in the form of a slave, offered himself for us in his passion in order to make us the body of this glorious head. . . . This is the sacrifice of Christians: we, being many, are one body in Christ. And this is also the sacrifice which the church continually celebrates in the sacrament of the altar, known to the faithful, in which the church teaches that it itself is offered in the offering it makes to God."[50]

In the Eucharist, the sacrifice of Christ and the "spiritual sacrifice" of the church become one because Christ takes the members of his body into the embrace of his sacrifice.

2. Imprinted without any problem in the memory of the West for centuries, this theme will often reappear in a polemical way at the time of the Reformation. The Anglican tradition introduced it into its liturgy: "And here we offer and present unto thee (O Lorde) oure selfe, oure souls, and bodies, to be a reasonable, holy, and liuely sacrifice unto thee."[51]

[49] Cyril of Alexandria, *On Haggai* 114, in *Sancti patris nostri Cyrilli archiepiscopi Alexandrini, In XII Prophetas*, 2 vols., ed. Philip Edward Pusey, (reprint, Brussels: Culture et civilisation, 1965) 2:268.

[50] Augustine, *The City of God* 10.6, in Schaff, 2:184, quoted at length in the preceding chapter, pp. 44–45.

[51] *The First and Second Prayer Books of Edward VI*, Everyman's Library 448 (New York: Dutton, 1932) 223.

Based on a text from Malachi (10:11),[52] many Fathers—perhaps already the *Didache*, Justin, then Irenaeus,[53] Tertullian[54]—and the liturgical anaphoras of the Eastern churches,[55] had identified the "spiritual sacrifice" with the Eucharist, "sacrifice of the New Covenant" offered in all places, "non-bloody holocaust." Justin did just that (ca. 150):

"As I said before, God has spoken through Malachi, one of the twelve prophets, about the sacrifices you formerly offered: 'I have no pleasure in you, says the Lord of hosts, and I will not accept an offering from your hands. For from the rising of the sun to its setting my name is great among the nations, and in every place incense is offered to my name, and a pure offering: for my name is great among the nations, says the Lord of hosts. But you profane it' [Malachi 1:10-12]. *And so God speaks of the Gentiles, namely us, who in every place offer God sacrifices, that is, the bread of the Eucharist and also the cup of the Eucharist*, affirming that we glorify the sacred name and you profane it."

And also:

"Accordingly, anticipating all the sacrifices we offer in this name, sacrifices Jesus Christ enjoined us to offer, *that is, the Eucharist of the bread and the cup*, and are presented by Christians everywhere throughout

---

[52] On this text from Malachi, see the very short but illuminating study of Karl Suso Frank, "Maleachi 1, 10ff in der frühen Väterdeeutung: Ein Beitrag zu Opferterminologie und Opferverständnis in der Alten Kirche," *Theologie und Philosophie* 53 (1978) 70–78.

[53] Justin, *Dialogue with Trypho* 28.5; 41.2; 116.3; 117.1; Irenaeus, *Against Heresies* 4.17.1, 5-6; 18.1. See *Didache* 14.3.

[54] Tertullian, *Against the Jews* 5.4-7; *Against Marcion* 3.22.6.

[55] Thus in the epiclesis of the anaphora of Chrysostom, from which we quoted just above: "We also offer you *this spiritual* and unbloody *worship,* and we invoke you, we pray you, we implore you to send your Holy Spirit on us and on these gifts presented to you and to make from this bread the precious body of your Christ, changing it by your Holy Spirit, [Amen], and [to make] from what is in this cup the precious blood of your Christ, changing it by your Holy Spirit, [Amen], so that they may be for those who will partake of them means to obtain sobriety of the soul, forgiveness of sins, reception of your Holy Spirit, fullness of the kingdom, free access to you, but not judgment and condemnation. We also offer you *this spiritual worship* for the fathers, patriarchs, prophets, apostles, preachers, evangelists, martyrs, confessors of the faith, virgins, and ascetics. . . ." Lodi, *Enchiridion,* nos. 2896–2901, 1271–81.

the world, God testifies that they are pleasing. *But God utterly rejects those that you and your priests offer* when the prophet says, 'I will not accept an offering from your hands. For from the rising of the sun to its setting my name is great among the nations. . . . But you profane it'" [Mal 1:10-12].[56]

We must especially recall the thought of Irenaeus, which was to be a determining factor in this domain, half a century after Justin, and must amply quote from *Against Heresies:*

"He took bread, provided by creation, and gave thanks and said, 'This is my body.' And likewise he declared the cup, also provided by creation, to which we all belong, his blood and *taught that it was the new oblation of the New Covenant. This is the oblation* the church received from the apostles and *throughout all the world* offers to God, who gives us as our nourishment *the firstfruits of God's own gifts under the New Covenant*. It was concerning this that Malachi, one of the twelve prophets, spoke beforehand: 'I have no pleasure in you, says the Lord of hosts, and I will not accept an offering from your hands. For from the rising of the sun to its setting my name is great among the nations, and *in every place* incense is offered to my name, and a pure offering; for my name is great among the nations, says the Lord of hosts' [Mal 1:10-12]. These words show in the most straightforward way *that the former people will cease to make offerings to God, but that in every place sacrifice will be offered to God, a pure one, and that the divine name will be glorified among the Gentiles.*

"But what other name is there which is glorified among the Gentiles except that of our Lord, by whom the Father is glorified and humanity as well? And because it is the name of God's own Son, whom God made flesh, God calls it God's own. . . . Therefore, since the name of the Son belongs to the Father, and since the church makes offerings to almighty God through Jesus Christ, God justly says for both these reasons, 'And in every place incense is offered to my name, and *a pure offering*' [Mal 1:11]. *Now, John declares in Revelation that this 'incense' is 'the prayers of the saints'* [5:8].

"*Accordingly, God accounts the oblation of the church, which the Lord instructed to be offered throughout all the world, as a pure and acceptable sacrifice.* It is not that God is in need of sacrifice from us, but that those

---

[56] Justin, *Dialogue with Trypho* 41.2–3; 117.1, in Roberts, 1:215, 257.

who offer are themselves glorified in what they do offer if their gift is accepted. *For by this gift we show both honor and affection for the Sovereign; and the Lord, wishing us to offer it in all simplicity and innocence,* said, 'So when you are offering your gift at the altar, if you remember that your brother or sister has something against you, leave your gift there before the altar and go; first be reconciled to your brother or sister, and then come and offer your gift' [Matt 5:23-24]. We are bound therefore *to offer to God the firstfruits of God's own creation,* as Moses says: 'They shall not appear before the Lord empty-handed,' [Deut 16:16] so that they, being accounted grateful because of the gifts by which they have shown their gratitude, may receive that honor which flows from God."[57]

That he is speaking of the Eucharist is proved by the continuation of his reasoning:

"But if any try to offer a sacrifice that is outwardly unexceptionable, correct, exact, while in their souls they do not share with their neighbors that communion which is just and fitting and do not possess the fear of God—they who thus cherish secret sin do not deceive God by that sacrifice which is offered with outward correctness; *nor will such an oblation profit them in any way, but only the renunciation of that evil conceived within them,* so that sin may no longer, by means of this hypocritical action, make them their own destroyers. . . .

"*Hence, sacrifices do not sanctify human beings, for God stands in no need of sacrifice; but the consciences of the offerers sanctify the sacrifice, when they are pure, and thus move God to accept it as from friends.* '[The sinner who] slaughters an ox is like . . . one who breaks a dog's neck' [Isa 66:3].

"Thus, *because the church offers with single-mindedness, its gift is justly reckoned a pure sacrifice in the eyes of God.* As Paul says to the Philippians, 'I am fully satisfied, now that I have received from Epaphroditus the gifts you sent, a fragrant offering, a sacrifice acceptable and pleasing to God' [Phil 4:18]. For we must make an oblation to God and in everything be grateful to God our Maker, *offering with a pure mind and a faith without hypocrisy, with well-grounded hope, and with fervent love the first-fruits of God's own created things. And the church alone offers this pure oblation to the Creator by offering with thanksgiving those things God's creation provides. . . .*

[57] Irenaeus, *Against Heresies* 4.17.5–18.1, in Roberts, 1:484.

"But none of the assemblies of heretics [offer this]. . . . *For how can they be certain within themselves that the bread over which thanks have been given is the body of their Lord and the cup his blood if they do not call him the Son of the Creator of the world, that is, the Word, through whom the wood fructifies, the springs gush forth, and the earth gives 'first the stalk, then the head, then the full grain in the head'* [Mark 4:28].

"Again, how can they say that the flesh, nourished by the body of the Lord and with his blood, is going to corrupt and not partake of life? *Therefore, let them either alter their opinion, or cease from offering the things just mentioned. But our opinion is in accordance with the Eucharist and the Eucharist in turn establishes our opinion.* For we offer God what is God's own, consistently proclaiming the communion and union of the flesh and Spirit. For as the bread, which comes from the earth, is no longer common bread when it receives the invocation of God, but the Eucharist, consisting of two realities, earthly and heavenly, so our bodies are no longer corruptible when they receive the Eucharist because they have the hope of the resurrection to eternity."

Irenaeus builds a synthesis of the Christian sacrifice around the Eucharist. He mentions especially the sacrifice of good deeds:

"We do not offer to God as if to someone in need, but to give thanks for God's gifts and thus sanctify creation. For just as God does not need our possessions, we need to offer something to God. As Solomon says, 'Whoever is kind to the poor / lends to God' [Prov 19:17]. *For God, who stands in need of nothing, accepts our good works in order to give us God's own good things in return.* As our Lord says: 'Come, you that are blessed by my Father, inherit the kingdom prepared for you . . . for *I was hungry and you gave me food, I was thirsty and you gave me something to drink, I was a stranger and you welcomed me, I was naked and you gave me clothing, I was sick and you took care of me, I was in prison and you visited me'* [Matt 25:34-36]. Thus, just as God has no need of these things yet desires them for our sake, *lest we be unfruitful,* the Word, in the same way, decreed that people make oblations, even though he had no need of them, *so that they might learn to serve God. And so it is his will that we also should offer a gift at the altar, frequently and without intermission.*

"The altar, then, is in heaven—our prayers and oblations are directed there—the temple likewise is there—as John says in Revelation, 'Then God's temple in heaven was opened' [11:19]—and the tabernacle as well—'See, the home of God is among mortals' [21:3]. The people received the gifts, oblations, and all the sacrifices as figures, conforming to what was shown Moses on the mountain, from the one same God, whose name is now glorified in the church among all nations."[58]

The intuition which Augustine will highlight is already present in Irenaeus; there is osmosis between "the firstfruits of God's own gifts under the New Covenant" (the bread and the cup which the Lord "declared . . . his blood" by making of it the "new oblation of the New Covenant" [4.17:5; 18:1]) and the inner quality of those who offer "the pure sacrifice."

The context underlines the necessity of the inner sacrifice, as the prophets had taught.[59] The authenticity of the Christians' action in *offering* "the firstfruits of the new creation" comes from the correspondence between what they are in their concrete lives and what they offer. They themselves must be "a new creation." Besides, if one must offer the bread "which creation provides" but is "[his] body," the cup "which creation provides" but is "[his] blood and the oblation of the New Covenant," it is so that the disciples themselves might be "neither unfruitful nor ungrateful."[60] It is imperative that their manner of living and thinking be in accord with the Eucharist and that the Eucharist in turn confirm their manner of living and thinking.[61] What counts above all is harmony—communion—between the offering and those who offer.

Irenaeus sees this harmony—this communion—even in the osmosis between the Lord's incorruptible body and the believers' body becoming incorruptible. What is offered and those who offer, now being "invested with new life," are in conformity with each other. The new life of the believers must be joined to the firstfruits of the new creation. Bread, wine, human beings are all taken up into the same and unique reality of the new world in its "fecundity," already at work.

---

[58] Ibid., 4.18.3–19.1, in Roberts, 1:485–86.

[59] Ibid., 4.14.1-3, in Roberts 1:478–79.

[60] Ibid., 4.17.5, in Roberts 1:484. Perhaps Jean de Watteville, *Le Sacrifice dans les textes eucharistiques des premiers siècles* (Neuchâtel: Delachaux et Niestlé, 1966) 93–102, does not stress sufficiently what to us is one of the principal components of Irenaeus' vision in this domain.

[61] See Irenaeus, *Against Heresies* 4.18.5, in Roberts, 1:485.

V. THE SACRIFICE OF PRAISE CULMINATING AT THE SYNAXIS

1. In the totality offered by the church at the Eucharist, praise holds a prominent place. When the New Testament speaks of the sacrifice of Christians, it does not mean just the "spiritual sacrifice" of a holy life seen as self-denial, practice of virtues, service to the neighbor. Hebrews states, "Through him, then, let us continually offer a sacrifice of praise to God, that is, the fruit of lips that confess his name" (Heb 13:15). For it is not enough, as a community, to serve others, the poor especially, through self-denial and to offer oneself as a member of the body or a branch of the vine. One must also be, with the others, *before God* in the confession of God's name and in praise. These demonstrate the *for God* of the sacrifice of a holy life, celebrated at the synaxis.

For his part, Paul in Galatians (2:19) and Romans (6:11) underlines the *for God* of life with Christ and the Spirit. In total communion with Christ Jesus—who, risen, lives *for God* (Rom 6:10)—believers "give as the sole object of their feelings, God, in God's justice, love, and grace as Christ revealed them."[62] Thus, they already live today "in [their] future," which is God, as Karl Barth comments. For

"[y]ou have no other choice! You have before you only life in communion with the One who has taken upon himself and done away with sin, your sin, and who has nothing before him but life with God. Such is the force of the imperative that commands your sanctification!"[63]

In this *for God*, the sacrifice of service to the poor in the denial of self for others and the daily acts of a holy life are, as it were, the parts of a choral whose melodic theme, unifying the whole composition and giving it its distinctive character, is gratuitous praise, thanksgiving, and the liturgical confession of the God and Father of Jesus.

2. When we presented the ideas of Philo—incontestably having affinities with certain circles of the New Testament—we remarked how the "spiritual sacrifice" of the holy life, which he so strongly emphasizes, does not constitute the whole of the worship which the people render to God. The liturgical worship of the Temple is also necessary. What is more, he sees there a form of service benefiting the

---

[62] Dodd, *Romans.*
[63] Karl Barth, *Petit commentaire de l'épître aux Romains* (Geneva, 1956) 68.

whole of humankind. For the thanksgiving offered in the Temple contributes to the cosmic justice on which the universe rests. In the place and for the good of all humanity, the people render the "service of God," which is part of the human vocation but about which few concern themselves.

"This is why it amazes me that some dare to charge the nation with an anti-social stance, a nation which has made such an extensive use of fellowship and goodwill toward all people everywhere that it offers up prayers and feasts and firstfruits on behalf of the whole human race and serves the truly self-existent God on behalf of themselves and others who have fled from the service they should have rendered."[64]

In any case, the "spiritual sacrifice" of a holy life itself is nourished and strengthened by the Temple worship:

"We ought to look upon the whole world as the highest and truest temple of God. For its most holy place it has that most sacred part of the essence of all existing things, heaven; for ornaments, the stars; and for priests, the angels, the subordinate ministers of his power, incorporeal souls, who are not compounded of irrational and rational natures as our bodies are, but having the irrational parts completely absent, are absolutely and wholly intellectual, pure intellects, resembling the monad.
"But the other temple is made with hands, for it was desirable not to cut short the impulses of people who were eager to bring in contributions for the objects of veneration and desirous either to show their gratitude by sacrifices for the good they had received or to implore pardon and forgiveness for whatever errors they might have committed. . . . For those who were not about to offer sacrifice in a pure and holy spirit would never endure quitting country, friends, and relations and emigrating into a distant land. But they would be likely, being under the influence of a more powerful attraction than that towards devotion, to remain attached to the society of their most intimate friends and relations who are like parts of themselves. And the most evident proof of this may be found in the events which actually took place.
"For innumerable companies of people from a countless variety of cities, some by land and some by sea, from east and from west, from north and from

---

[64] Philo, *Special Laws* 2.167, in Philo, *Works*, 584.

south, came to the Temple at every festival, as if to some common refuge and safe asylum from the troubles of this most busy and painful life. There, they sought to find tranquillity and remission and respite from those cares which from their earliest infancy had hampered and weighed them down, and catching their breath, as it were, they sought *to pass a brief time in cheerful festivities. Filled with good hopes, they enjoyed the leisure of that most important and necessary vacation which consists in forming a friendship with those hitherto unknown. But now, aroused by boldness and a desire to honor God and forming a union of actions and natures, they joined in sacrifices and libations, the most complete confirmation of mutual good will.*"[65]

The necessary complementarity between "spiritual sacrifice" of a holy life and "sacrifice of praise" of the cultic liturgy is explicitly attested by Hebrews. According to it, the "sacrifices" that please God are both those of the confession of God's name and those of mutual charity (Heb 13:15-16).[66] But the idea of the "sacrifice of praise" is present throughout the whole New Testament, if only in the precept to live in thanksgiving, which is a distinctive element of Christian identity. The habitual disposition of the faithful, who acknowledge God and, "remembering" God's kindnesses toward them, feel thankfulness and praise well up within themselves, must pass from the heart to the lips. Earlier, a text of Hosea, which the Septuagint transmits in a sense different from the Hebrew original (14:3), said this, "Take with you words . . . speak to him . . . we will render in return the fruit of our lips."[67] The phrase "fruit of the lips" was known at Qumran.[68] As for Psalm 50, which also proclaims that holocausts of bulls and rams are useless, it placed the following words in God's mouth, "Offer to God a sacrifice of thanksgiving," "Those who bring thanksgiving as their sacrifice honor me" (Ps 50:14, 23).

[65] Ibid., 1.66-69, in ibid., 540.

[66] Donald Guthrie, *The Epistle to the Hebrews: An Introduction and Commentary*, 3 vols., Tyndale New Testament Commentaries 15 (1961–1965; reprint, Grand Rapids, Mich.: Eerdmans, 1986) 276.

[67] See Philip Edgecumbe Hughes, *A Commentary on the Epistle to the Hebrews* (Grand Rapids, Mich.: Eerdmans, 1977) 583–84; Frederick F. Bruce, *Commentary on the Epistle to the Hebrews*, New London Commentaries on the New Testament (London: Marshall, Morgan and Scott, 1965) 405–6.

[68] *Hymns* 1.28; *Rule of the Community* 9.4 (*IQS* 9.4-5; *IQH* 1.28). See Menahem Mansoor, "Thanksgiving Hymns and Masoretic Text," *Revue de Qumrân* 3 (1961–1962) 387–94.

The word *todah* is important. For on the one hand, the Septuagint translates it by "sacrifice of praise" *(thusia aineseōs)*—an expression found later on in Hebrews 13:15, but already used elsewhere[69]—on the other hand, some translators, Aquila among them, translate it by *eucharistia*. And it is clear that when Philo uses the word *eucharistia*, he has *todah* in mind.[70] This word has the precise meaning of praise-filled proclamation of God's deeds, anamnesis full of admiration and thankfulness for the *mirabilia Dei* (marvelous deeds of God). The word had come to sometimes designate one of the three great sacrifices of communion in which a meal is shared with God, one part being consumed by fire on the altar and the other given back, replete with divine blessing, to those who had offered it. An offering of cakes and breads, one of which is taken "for God," is often added to the ritual. Thus, the "sacrifice of the lips" and the liturgical rite of the "communion meal" are intermingled into a total expression of the believers' attitude of thankfulness and praise *before God*.

But the *todah* is wider in scope than this specific case.[71] It is the basic attitude of believers whose hearts, purified (by the "spiritual sacrifice of a holy life"), *remember* God, acknowledge the overwhelming gratuitousness of salvation, and express by their praise the feelings that this realization has aroused in their hearts. As Augustine said:

"I must return to myself, where I will find what I will immolate; I must return to myself; in myself I will find the sacrifice of praise. Let my conscience be your altar. . . . O gratuitous sacrifice, given by grace! Indeed, I have not bought this to offer; you have given it, for I would not even have this. And this is the immolation of the sacrifice of

[69] Thus Ps 26:7; Ps 50:14; Ps 107:22; 115:8 (LXX); 116:17; Lev 7:13, 15; 2 Chr 29:31; 1 Macc 4:56.

[70] Laporte, *Doctrine eucharistique*, 43–45; Henri Cazelles, "L'Anaphore de l'Ancien Testament," in *Eucharisties d'Orient et d'Occident*, 2 vols., Semaine liturgique de l'institut Saint-Serge, Lex Orandi 46 (Paris: Cerf, 1970) 11–21 (16–17); Cazelles, "Eucharistie, bénédiction et sacrifice dans l'Ancien Testament," *MD* 123 (1975) 7–28 (22–24).

[71] On the *todah*, besides the studies of Cazelles mentioned in the note above, see Roland de Vaux, *Les sacrifices de l'Ancien Testament*, Les Cahiers de la revue biblique 1 (Paris: Gabalda, 1964) 7–27 (33); Suzanne Daniel, *Recherches sur le vocabulaire du culte dans la Septante* (Paris: Klincksieck, 1966) 273–77; Charles Perrot, "Le Repas du Seigneur," *MD* 123 (1975) 29–46; Thomas J. Talley, "De la *Berakah* à l'Eucharistie," *MD* 125 (1976) 11–37. See the older but still useful study of Charles Jouon, "Reconnaissance et remerciement en hébreu classique," *Biblica* 4 (1923) 381–85.

praise, to render thanks to the One from whom you have whatever good you have. . . . *Immolate to God the sacrifice of praise.*"[72]

3. When one attentively ponders the New Testament passages in which *eucharistein* and its derivatives *eucharistia* and *eucharistos* are used according to the custom of the translators and Philo, one realizes that, indeed, these terms express the fundamental stance of believers before God. Here is the root of their response to the grace received from God. Paul says this clearly to the Corinthians, "Yes, everything [that servants of the gospel experience] is for your sake, so that grace, as it extends to more and more people, may increase *thanksgiving*, to the glory of God" (2 Cor 4:15). Moreover, what Christians do for others, in particular by being concerned for the poorest and sharing with them, has here its ultimate purpose: "for the rendering of this ministry [for the church of Jerusalem, which is in dire straits] not only supplies the needs of the saints but also overflows with many *thanksgivings* to God" (2 Cor 9:12); "[it] will produce *thanksgiving* to God through us" (2 Cor 9:11). This thanksgiving goes far beyond gratitude for the money received. It reaches as far as faith and obedience to the gospel, which inspire generosity, as far as the sense of communion, which is at the heart of the Christian experience (2 Cor 9:13). It is therefore the whole impact of the work of God on the Corinthians' lives which becomes the object of *eucharistia*. "Self-denial," "spiritual sacrifice of a holy life," "sacrifice of good deeds" are integrated into the "sacrifice of praise" (*todah* according to the translation of the Septuagint followed by Heb 13:15) and the "sacrifice of the lips."

The same is true of Paul when he contemplates the progress of evangelization. He transforms into thanksgiving his gratitude and his joy before God (Rom 1:8-9; 1 Thess 3:9-10). Besides, what God wants, in Christ, is that believers—on whom God lavishes benefactions—may "*give thanks* in all circumstances" (1 Thess 5:18). One should not be surprised then that Colossians enjoins upon the faithful the precept of thanksgiving (Col 2:7) and further on specifies, "And whatever you do, in word or in deed, do everything in the name of the Lord Jesus, *giving thanks* to God the Father through him" (Col 3:17), as well as, "Devote yourselves to prayer, keeping alert in it with *thanksgiving*" (Col 4:2). The faithfulness of believers to this precept is a response to

---

[72] *Exp on Ps* 50 [49].21, in Schaff, 8:185.

the benevolence of God, communion with God's plan unfolding through the length of days.

Very early on, the Christian community was aware that its *eucharistia* can be genuine only "in Christ" and it accorded a particular place to its own communion to Jesus' supreme *eucharistia,* that in which the farewell meal unfolded. There, the *eucharistia* of his entire life was, as it were, gathered and concentrated. But it was then associated with a ritual, the ritual of the bread and cup in a "liturgy of the meals" which, in the Jewish tradition, was always accomplished in a climate of thanksgiving.

In Jesus' time, the meals comprised a blessing *(berakah)*, a thanksgiving, and an appeal to God's mercy.[73] The stories of the Last Supper transmitted by the gospel traditions preserve the indication that Jesus pronounced the blessing on the bread (Matt 26:26; Mark 14:22), gave thanks over the cup (Matt 26:27; Mark 14:23; Luke 22:17; 1 Cor 11:25) and the bread (Luke 22:19; 1 Cor 11:25). Whereas the terms "to bless, "to pronounce the blessing" (in Greek *eulogein, eulogia)* correspond to the Hebrew words from the root *barak (berakah, berakoth)*, the expression "to give thanks" corresponds to *todah,* whose meaning it keeps.[74] Now, if the "blessing" (to God) is essentially an expression of admiration and joy before the wonderful works of God and the grandeur of God's plan, the "thanksgiving" *(eucharistia)* is above all a response

[73] See Talley, *"Berakah"* 15–37; Louis Finkelstein, "The *Birkat hamazon*," *Jewish Quarterly Review* 19 (1928–1929) 211–62. Here are these prayers in their short version: "1. May you be blessed, Lord our God, king of the universe, you who feed the whole world with kindness, grace, and mercy./ May you be blessed, Lord, you who give food to all beings.// 2. We give you thanks, Lord, our God, because you gave us as a heritage a good and pleasant land, the Covenant, the Law, life, and food./ For all these things we give you thanks and we praise your name forever./ May you be blessed, Lord, for the land and the food.// 3. Have mercy, Lord our God, on Israel your people, on Jerusalem your city, on your Temple the place where you dwell, on Zion the place of your rest, on the great and holy sanctuary for which your name is invoked, and deign in our time to restore in its proper place the kingdom and the dynasty of David, and soon rebuild Jerusalem./ May you be blessed, Lord, who build Jerusalem."

[74] On this subject see, in connection with the discussion provoked by the opinions of Jean-Paul Audet in "Esquisse historique du genre littéraire de la Bénédiction juive et de l'Eucharistie chrétienne," *RB* 65 (1958) 371–99, and in *La Didaché, instructions des apôtres,* Études bibliques (Paris: Galalda, 1958) 372–433, the studies of Talley, *"Berakah,"* 19–22, 35–37; Cazelles, "Anaphore et l'Ancien Testament," 18–28; Robert J. Ledogar, *Acknowledgment: Praise Verbs in the Early Greek Anaphora* (Rome, Herder, 1968) 115–24; and Perrot "Repas du Seigneur," 30.

filled with gratitude, proceeding from the innermost recesses of the individual and community as redeemed people. They turn to God in offering the "sacrifice of the lips" which becomes the thanksgiving due to God. This is why the *eucharistia* is structured around the remembrance of what God has done, the memory which is in its very nature the authentic "confession of faith." All that believing people keep in their *memory* is proclaimed in an anamnesis of the marvels effected by God, a discourse which is a "work of glory." Irenaeus said that the "eucharistied" cup is like the compendium of the whole story of salvation (*Against Heresies* 3.11.5; 3.16.7).

At the Last Supper, Jesus "gave thanks" over the cup, say all the witnesses, on the bread and the cup, says the tradition preserved by Paul and Luke. And since, at that period, the content of the "thanksgiving" was still "living and flexible,"[75] one can think that Jesus imbued it with the sense of his mission, conscious as he was of the deep reality of the Covenant and of the imminence of his death:[76]

"The pericope of Emmaus offers us perhaps indications that suggest the same thing: the disciples would have recognized the Lord (Luke 24:31) by his prayer of thanksgiving at the breaking of the bread. It is possible that Jesus had not chosen the traditional formula of the Jewish prayers to give thanks at the Last Supper; indeed, they were no longer suited to the newness of the Last Supper, all imbued with fullness and completion. Perhaps we can interpret the words of Jesus at the Last Supper as an echo of his prayer of thanksgiving that had just preceded them. In this prayer Jesus would perhaps have given thanks for the salvation being effected at that very moment, for the gift of his body and of his bloody death, for the New Covenant being inaugurated now, for the future banquet in the reign of God, for his resurrection at hand, for the imminent coming of the reign of God. If Jesus had really used a personal expression for his prayer of thanksgiving, one could, by the same token, explain also the primitive custom allowing those who spoke in tongues to give free expression to their thanksgiving (*Didache* 10.7; compare 1 Cor 14:16).

"In several places of the apostolic writings, one hardly can help thinking that the idea of the eucharistic prayer has had an influence

[75] Talley, "*Berakah*," 20.

[76] See what Heinz Schürmann says of Jesus' actions at the Last Supper in *Comment Jésus a-t-il vécu sa mort?: Exégèse et théologie*, trans. Albert Chazelle, Lectio divina 93 (Paris, Cerf: 1977) 97–116.

on the formulation of the texts (see especially Eph 5:20; Col 3:17; 1 Thess 5:18). If one wants to get an approximate idea of the eucharistic prayers of the early church, it would be necessary to study the great prayers of thanksgiving which introduce Paul's letters and the hymns in John's Revelation."[77]

The Christians' daily thanksgiving to the Father, always done "in Christ" (Rom 1:8; 7:25; Eph 5:20; Col 3:17), certainly found in the Sunday communion with the Lord's thanksgiving during the Last Supper its moment of plenitude and fellowship. Ordinarily dispersed in time and space, the community was then able *as such* to "give thanks" to the Father (to make Eucharist) in the thanksgiving of the Lord himself. And this it did at the very moment when it "remembered" his farewell meal, assured that the Spirit gave in the bread and the cup a share of the body and the blood delivered for the gathering together of humankind. In this "thanksgiving" *(eucharistia)* it was able *as community* to confess together, to announce *(katangellein,* 1 Cor 11:26) with the ritual gestures and words of its anamnesis both the marvel of Christ's pasch and the wonderful works of God reaching their climax in it. Thus, the "daily sacrifice" of its praise and thanksgiving—accomplished by its dispersed members, in anonymity and often silence—was expressed in a single "sacrifice of the lips," a single *todah* to the praise of God "in Christ."

After the *Didache,* Ignatius of Antioch is the witness of the importance that very early (ca. 100), the church gave to this thanksgiving *(eucharistia):* "Take care, then, to come together often to give God thanks *(eucharistia)* and praise." For Ignatius, this word has already come to designate the whole ritual: "Take care to have but one Eucharist. For there is one flesh of our Lord Jesus Christ, and one cup of our unity in his blood; one altar; one bishop along with the presbytery and deacons."[78] Justin is perhaps clearer:

"Now, I also admit that prayers and thanksgiving, when offered by worthy people, are the only perfect and pleasing sacrifices to God. For these alone are what Christians have undertaken to offer; and in the remembrance effected by their food and drink, they commemorate the suffering of the Son of God which He endured [for them]. . . ."[79]

[77] Schürmann, *Le Récit,* 41.

[78] Ignatius of Antioch, Letter to the Ephesians 13.1, in Roberts, 1:55; Letter to the Philadelphians 4, in ibid., 1:81; see Letter to the Smyrneans 7.1; 8.1, in ibid., 1:89–90.

[79] Justin, *Dialogue with Trypho* 117.2-3, in Roberts, 1:257.

In Alexandria, Origen (ca. 250) also declares:

"But we, while recognizing the duty of thankfulness, maintain that we show no ingratitude by refusing to give thanks to beings who do us no good, but who rather set themselves against us when we neither sacrifice to them nor worship them. We are much more concerned lest we should be ungrateful [acharistoi] to God, who has loaded us with God's benefits, whose work we are, who cares for us, whatever our station, and who has given us hopes of things beyond this present life. And we have a symbol of gratitude [tēs eucharistias] to God in the bread which we call the Eucharist."[80]

Eusebius of Caesarea (d. 340) finds images showing the close connection between the different levels of the Christian "sacrifice":

"We sacrifice to almighty God a sacrifice of praise. We sacrifice the divine, holy, and sacred offering. We sacrifice the pure sacrifice anew according to the New Covenant. . . . Yes, and we offer the incense announced by the prophet, everywhere bringing God the sweet-smelling fruit of the sincere word of God, offering it in our prayers to God. . . . So, then, we sacrifice and offer incense: we celebrate the memorial of the great sacrifice according to the mysteries delivered to us, and bring to God the thanksgiving [eucharistian] for our salvation with holy hymns and prayers; at the same time, we consecrate ourselves to God alone and to the Word, God's high priest, devoted to God body and soul."[81]

And here, once again, Augustine reflects with his customary depth on the universal faith, especially in the chapter of *The City of God* from which we already have quoted several excerpts:

"We owe God the service which in Greek is called latreia, *whether we render it outwardly or inwardly; for we are all God's temple, each of us individually and all of us together* because God consents to inhabit *each individually and the whole harmonious body,* and is no more in all than in each, since

---

[80] Origen, *Against Celsus* 8.57, in *PG* 11, 1604.

[81] Eusebius *Proof of the Gospel* 1.10, in Eusebius of Caesarea, *The Proof of the Gospel*, ed. and trans. W. J. Ferrar (1920; reprint Grand Rapids, Mich.: Baker, 1982) 62; [adapted by the editor].

God is neither made larger nor divided. Our heart when it rises to God is God's altar; the priest who intercedes for us is God's Only-Begotten; we sacrifice bleeding victims to God when we contend for divine truth even to the shedding of our blood; we offer the sweetest incense to God when we come before God burning with holy and pious love; we dedicate and surrender ourselves and God's gifts to us. *In solemn feasts and on appointed days, we consecrate to God the memory of God's benefits,* lest through the lapse of time ungrateful oblivion should steal upon us; *on the altar of our heart we offer God the sacrifice of humility and praise, kindled by the fire of burning love.* We are cleansed from all stain of sin and evil passions and are consecrated in God's name so that we may see God, so far as God can be seen; so that we may cleave to Him. . . .

"It follows that the whole redeemed city, that is, the assembly or community of the saints, is offered to God as our sacrifice through the great high priest who, in the form of a slave, offered himself for us in his passion in order to make us the body of this glorious head. . . .

"This is the sacrifice of Christians: *we, being many, are one body in Christ. And this is also the sacrifice which the church continually celebrates in the sacrament of the altar, known to the faithful, in which the church teaches that it itself is offered in the offering it makes to God.*"[82]

4. In the "sacrament of the altar" the various "sacrifices" are thus together in osmosis. All of them are embraced by the sacramental presence of the paschal sacrifice which Christ offered "once for all" and in which all the forms of his own sacrifice found their fulfillment: "sacrifice of good deeds and mutual help," "spiritual sacrifice of a holy life," "sacrifice of praise," "sacrifice of the lips," particularly sacrifice of one's own life. Then, in virtue of their entering into the power of the paschal sacrifice of communion of Christ, the hearts and words of those whom the synaxis assembles form a unique and radically indivisible "sacrifice," that of the church, body and head.

Indeed, it is the Christian community *as such* which, through the minister—the sign in its midst of the Lord gathering his own—"renders thanks" to God "in Christ." We do not have here anything like a sheaf of eucharists which would be tied together by the word of the president. On the contrary, it is at the Eucharist that through the ministry of the bishop or presbyter, the body of Christ calls forth the

---

[82] Augustine, *City of God* 10.3, 6, in Schaff, 2:182, 183–84.

common thanksgiving of the body of Christ, of the vine of the Lord in which every person communicates in faith. For every participant must strive to let himself or herself be fashioned by the "thanksgiving" of the church. This thanksgiving is neither one's property nor "the fruit of anyone's lips" even though that person might be the president at the synaxis. It is larger than anyone, is not always in accord with one's inner state of mind, proclaims praise when one might be in distress and in tears, is concerned only with the wonderful works of God revealed in Scripture, whereas one might prefer to confess the marvels accomplished by God in one's personal life. It is the common possession of the body *as such*.

Through the AMEN that concludes the anaphora, the community *as such* solemnly affixes the seal of its faith on what the minister has proclaimed. This AMEN is very rich. Justin mentions it twice: "When [the president] has concluded the prayers and thanksgivings, all the people present express their assent by saying Amen" and "The president likewise offers as best one can prayers and thanksgiving, and the people assent with Amen."[83] What is more, in the early centuries there seems to be the conviction that every baptized person has an inalienable right to hear the thanksgiving, join in repeating AMEN, stand by the table and hold out his or her hands to receive the blessed food, and partake of the body and blood of our Lord Jesus Christ.[84] This is probably why, when in subsequent times the Canon will be pronounced in a low voice, at least the final doxology will still be said aloud in order to allow the response AMEN. Augustine, who sees in the AMEN the *subscriptio* (signature) of faith,[85] affirms that in eternal life *"tota actio nostra AMEN et ALLELUIA"* (our whole activity will consist of AMEN and ALLELUIA),[86] an eternal and praise-filled acquiescence to what God is, sung by the choir of the blessed and not by isolated voices. Eternal life will be rooted in this "AMEN, *it was* true, *it is* true" of the ecclesial *communion as such*.

[83] Justin, *First Apology* 65.4; 67.4, in Roberts, 1:185–86.

[84] See the letter of Dionysius, recorded by Eusebius, *History of the Church* 7.1.4, in Schaff and Wace, 1:297.

[85] "Amen vestrum, subscriptio vestra est, consensio vestra, adstipulatio vestra est" (Your amen is your signature, your consent, your agreement). This is a fragment of a sermon, *Against Pelagius* 3, in PL 39:1721; see also "Amen" in *Jahrbuch für Antike und Christentum* 1 (1958) 153–59.

[86] Augustine, *Sermon* 362.29-31, in Hill, 3:265.

5. And so the AMEN of the anaphoras of the earthly liturgy reveals that it is a sacramental communion with the AMEN of the eternal liturgy. The one "thanksgiving" of the church of God, in the unique sacrifice into which the community gathered here and now fully enters, is sung on our earth in communion, not only with the other local churches which also celebrate the same sacrifice within their own context, but with the heavenly church.

When Revelation presents the eternal liturgy, it does so in an essentially sacrificial language with biblical overtones. Everything takes place around the throne where the Lamb is identified with the Living One for all eternity (5:12, 13; 7:14; 14:1-5; 19:11; 21:23; 22:1-3). The gift he makes of himself is unceasingly alluded to (5:9; 14:4). Those whom the Lamb has redeemed from among human beings share in this liturgy because the holiness of their lives was manifested in particular in "the great ordeal" (7:4; 14:4-5; 19:8). Their prayers are the incense of the sacrifice (5:8; 8:3). Their song is a pure *eucharistia* focused on the marvels of the salvation won by the Lamb:

"You are worthy to take the scroll
    and to open its seals,
for you were slaughtered and by your blood you ransomed for God
    saints from every tribe and language and people and nation;
you have made them to be a kingdom of priests serving our God,
    and they will reign on earth" (5:9-10; see 4:11; 7:12; 14:3).

The *Amen* and the *Alleluia* of this liturgy punctuate the worship they celebrate "day and night within his temple" (7:15; see 11:1-2; 21:22), a temple which is no other than "the Lord God the Almighty and the Lamb" (21:22) since there is no longer any material temple in the eternal city. The church of heaven is the church in a state of sacrifice, the church which is no longer anything but the "sacrifice of a holy life" consummated in glory, in the eternal *eucharistia* of the living God, the church fully itself.

When, on earth, a local church celebrates the meal of Christ, it does nothing less than anticipate and reflect in the moving flux of history the sacrifice which is the reality of its eternal life. This is why the Eucharist is, in the richest meaning of the term, the sacrifice of the church of God.

VI. THE SACRIFICE OF FAITH

1. Philo had seen in the faith of the people of God the sacrifice par excellence. The Letter to the Philippians is the echo of this conviction in the consciousness of the Christian community. To its addressees it speaks of the sacrifice *(thusia)* of their faith (2:17). The context is illuminating.

In the same way as the libations are poured over the sacrificial victims, the blood which Paul would pour out in his martyrdom would be as a libation over the sacrifice of his Christians' faith: "But even if I am being poured out as a libation over the sacrifice and the offering *(leitourgia)* of your faith, I am glad and rejoice with all of you." There is communion of the two sacrifices—that of martyrdom and that of faith—but of the two, the second is the more important since it is as the raison d'être of the first.[87]

It is evident that we deliberately end our presentation of the sacrificial nature of ecclesial life with the eminent place of the "sacrifice of faith." For all Christian sacrifices—from that of self-denial, of concern for the poor, of service, of martyrdom, of holy life, of praise, of the *eucharistia*, to that of the eternal liturgy—have their source in the sacrifice of faith. To come back to our image, it is the warp on which all the other threads are woven. A detailed exegetical study of the liturgical sections in Revelation reveals that for their author or compiler, the liturgy of the heavenly *eucharistia* is the consummation in glory of the faith of the church on its journey. And its AMEN (3:14), which comes to designate Christ himself in a letter written "on the Lord's day" (1:10) remains radically unintelligible without reference to the word of God and the witness of Jesus Christ (1:2, 9; 6:9; 12:17; 19:10; 20:4). Besides, at the opening of the fifth seal, the author sees "under the altar the souls of those who had been slaughtered for the word of God and for the testimony they had given" and who receive a white robe while they wait for the number of their fellow servants and of those destined to be martyrs to be complete (6:9-11). The immense throng at the liturgy of the throne are the believers "who have come out of the great

---

[87] Translators hesitate on the meaning of *leitourgia*. The *obsequium fidei* [service of faith—service in the sense of duty rendered out of faith. Trans.] of the Vulgate will become a classical formula in the West. But very often, the "*sacrificium* of faith" will disappear from the theological commentaries and only the *obsequium fidei* will be retained, a phrase which modern languages do not always know how to render.

ordeal; they have washed their robes and made them white in the blood of the Lamb. / For this reason they are before the throne of God, / and worship him day and night within his temple" (7:14-15). Without faith, lived and confessed in historical time, there is no eternal sacrifice of praise, no *eucharistia* of the church.

2. The sacrifice of the church on all its levels is based on the sacrifice of faith. For faith is the decision to totally trust God with one's life, with the meaning of one's life, with one's final beatitude. It is a "sacrifice" not because it would demand either the denial of understanding and lead to drowning in irrationality, even absurdity, or the refusal to live life in its fullness. On the contrary, it is a "sacrifice" because it recognizes in the fullness of life the fruit of welcoming God's gratuitous gift. And this welcome is glorification of the Father in Christ and the Spirit.

Because by their faith, Christians welcome the limitless *agapē* of the Father's plan, they practice the sacrifice of hospitality, of almsgiving, of service. Matthew's pericope of the Last Judgment (v. 25-31) and the brief remark in the Hebrews about those who have "entertained angels" (13:2) are laden with meaning. Believers do not know who the real object of their generosity is, whereas this object is, in fact, "the Christ of God." They offer a sacrifice in the strength of their faith in the precept of love. It is also in the strength of their faith that they accept to lay down their lives, assured that what God has done "in Christ" reveals the value of the sacrifice of one's life. It is also in the strength of their faith that they set their foot on the narrow path, traced by the gospel, of a life in which the Father is glorified because then, "the work of God's hands" responds to God's desire. In the sacrifice of praise and the liturgical *eucharistia*, it is obvious that the object is the memorial of what faith receives as a revelation of the God and Father of Jesus Christ and of his work. The church of God is built on the rock of faith. Must we remind readers that this faith is always transmitted by the other who announces it (Rom 10:14-15), from the apostolic community and before that, the prophets? Faith is spread by the mission, by those who are sent.

3. In this perspective, the question of the relationship between faith and works is singularly clarified, as well as the sacrificial scope of the Eucharist. The Letter of James attests to the fecundity and absolute primacy of faith when it says, "What good is it . . . if you say you

have faith but do not have works?" (2:14). Furthermore, several apostolic statements echo this, including some in the Pauline corpus.[88]

It is perhaps the Letter to Titus which contains the most balanced formula on the topic of works: "He it is who gave himself for us that he might redeem us from all iniquity and purify for himself a people of his own who are zealous for good deeds [kalōn ergōn]" (2:14). Salvation is a gratuitous gift of the agapē of God, through the sacrifice of Christ Jesus (his delivering up his own self). This gift is received by faith transmitted by the Word (see Titus 2:15). The Spirit does this in order that the Word may produce in believers what John's Gospel calls "much fruit" (15:8; see 15:2), "fruit that will last" (15:16); what Matthew's Gospel calls "a hundredfold . . . sixty . . . thirty" (13:23). Gift and fruit call for one another. The fruit glorifies the gift, revealing its fecundity.

The fruit comes from God alone (John 15:5). However, through sheer grace, it consists in *the works* of the sacrifice of a holy life whose dynamism is that of the Spirit gratuitously given along with faith. The Johannine tradition simultaneously states, "This is *the work* of God, that you believe in him whom he has sent" (6:29) and, "The one who believes in me will also do *the works* that I do and, in fact, will do greater works than these, because I am going to the Father" (14:12). The passage from *the work* to *the works* perfectly expresses the relationship between faith and the other forms of sacrifice (self-denial, holy life, liturgy); the latter, accomplished in freedom, are the sanctifying marks of the former. The *work* of God is that which fructifies into *works*, usually aiming at benefitting others.

The Pauline thought especially stresses the link of causality between the one sacrifice of Christ offered "once for all" *(ephapax)* and the sacrifices of a holy life. Because of both faith and baptism, which is its sacrament, believers become, "in Christ," an altar, as it were, to God.[89] Hence, the work accomplished in conformity with this communion with Christ is a sacrifice offered to God (Rom 12:1). Readers will

[88] Thus Rom 2:6, 15-16; Gal 5:6; Col 1:10; Eph 2:8-10; Titus 2:14; 1 Thess 1:3; 2 Thess 1:11. See Matt 5:16, 20; 7:12-27; 12:50; 18:23-35; 25:31-36.

[89] These lines had been already written when we found almost identical expressions in the article of Sylvie Anne Goldberg, "La Famille juive: réalisation du projet divin," *ARM* 79 (1990) 27–28. This similarity—which is not without connection with what we have said about Philo's thought and the New Testament—is in our opinion quite significant and very important in helping to clarify the thorny question of works.

remember that this was Augustine's explanation. But one can also say, with Chrysostom, that every action offered on this altar (above all, on that part of the altar which is the poor whom one venerates, serves, and honors) is a sacrifice to God, offered not in addition to the sacrifice of Christ but *"in him,"* "in Christ" and "in the Spirit."[90]

4. When he treats of the Eucharist, Augustine bequeaths to Western tradition a sophisticated view of the relation between word and bread. "Eating the word" at the synaxis is inseparable from "eating the eucharistic bread." The two are in symbiosis. One cannot eat the flesh of the Lord in truth without at the same time "eating" the word. Christ is life-giving food only inasmuch as he is inseparably both the sacramental body consecrated by the Spirit and the word of faith, received in the mouth and eaten in the heart. Augustine's statements are well known: "It is not what we see but what we believe that nourishes us"; "Do not open your mouth but your heart"; "When we receive him, we know what we are thinking"; "We receive a small amount and are fattened by the heart"; *"Crede et manducasti* [believe, and you have eaten]."[91]

The word announced and received is therefore essential for the church. To highlight the eucharistic character of the word does not in the least relativize its role. Word and sacrament together form communion. The sacrament arises within the word, and within the genesis of the church. Word and faith are always first.

[90] Concerning the question of the poor, which we have had to treat quite briefly, see especially, from the angle we are interested in, Francis J. Moloney, "The Eucharist as Jesus' Presence to the Broken," *Pacifica* (Pacifica Theological Studies Assn.) 2 (1989) 151–74; Bernard Coulié, *Les Richesses dans l'œuvre de saint Grégoire de Nazianze: Étude littéraire et historique* (Louvain-la-Neuve: Catholic University of Louvain, 1985); Adalbert-G. Hamman and France Quéré-Jaulmes, *Riches et pauvres dans l'Église ancienne* (Paris: Grasset, 1982); Jean-Marie-Roger Tillard, *La Pauvreté religieuse, choisir entre Dieu et Mammon* (Ottawa, 1985, duplicated).

[91] The connection between faith and baptism is remarkably expressed by Ambrose, *On the Mysteries* 19–28, in *Des Sacrements*, rev. ed., trans. and ed. Bernard Botte, SC 25 bis, 164–70 [also in *On the Sacraments*]: "You confessed your faith in the Son, your faith in the Holy Spirit. Remember the order of these facts. *In this faith,* you have died to the world and have risen to God; you have been buried, as it were, in this element of the world; "dead to sin" [Rom 6:11], you are raised to eternal life. *Believe, therefore, that this water is not without power."* As for Augustine's texts on the connection between faith and baptism, see especially *Homilies on the Gospel of John* 25.12, in Schaff, 7:164–65; 26.12, in Schaff, 7:171–72; *Sermon 71.17*, in Hill, 3:255–56; *Sermon 112.5*, in Hill, 4:149–50; *Sermon 131.1*, in Hill 4:316–17.

The advent of communion in no way contradicts the normal law of the economy *(oikonomia)* according to which the work of God has its foundation in the word. The people are a people of the word. It is the word which tells the people what the divine plan is, and it is in the voice and writings of the prophets—who are its channels—that this plan is shown to be inseparable from the demands associated with salvation. Matthew's Gospel ends with the command to teach all the nations; the first chapters of Acts depict the apostles announcing the gospel of God to the Jews, then to the pagans; Paul defines himself as the one God sends to preach; John's Gospel opens with a long disquisition on the *Logos* and its work. The church—whose communion the Eucharist will seal—is at first in gestation, then born in the word, under the power of the Spirit. It was the grace of the Reformation to remind the West of this. The point of departure for the church is the *sacrificium verbi* (the sacrifice of the word). Hence the importance of the mission.

However, the word becomes life-giving dynamism with the Spirit only, in fact, when the community—the one which the synaxis gathers and binds together—knows how to make of the word, not a sacred book kept in archives, but an ever timely reality challenging humankind at the most intimate place of its hopes and failures, its joys and tears, its happiness and pain. This cannot be done in solitude. It is the mission of the people of God *as such*, with the complementarity of its functions and charismas, of the *sensus fidelium* (the insight of the faithful) and the hierarchical ministries, of the Christians who show a peaceful faithfulness and those who are continually in need of forgiveness, of those who are never shaken in their convictions and those who are tormented by anxiety, of those who have never betrayed and those who are aware of their kinship with the prodigal son. Where can this people be gathered together if not at the synaxis, by word and sacrament?

At the root of the church of God, word and sacrament are one whole. Without the word and the faith it arouses, the sacrament is only an empty ritual; without the Eucharist, the word does not lead believers into the depths of the "mystery." It is not by accident that the reaffirmation of the ecclesiology of communion at Vatican II coincided with the rediscovery of the role of the word and the renewal of the mission.

VII. THE SACRIFICE: THE CHURCH OF GOD

1. And so we arrive at the conclusion of this reflection on the sacrifice of the church. We have seen that the Eucharist and the church are

in symbiosis, in the dynamism of the Word and Spirit. The church is born of God's gift received by faith in the power of the Spirit. The Eucharist is *this gift* in its totality communicated by the Spirit to the community in order that this community, throughout its whole life, may be in truth, already on earth and later on in eternal glory, what the word announces, demands, and promises: a *sacrifice* of peace and joy to the glory of our God and Father, a sacrifice offered through Christ, with him and in him, by the church entirely incorporated into his pasch.

The relation between believers and God is necessarily inserted into this relation between *sacrifice* and church, without being in the least denied or obscured. And this goes for prayer even though it is the most secret possession of Christians. Commenting on the Our Father, Cyprian is able to write:

"Before all things, the Teacher of peace and the Master of unity would not have prayer said individually and privately, as if one prayed for herself or himself alone. . . . Our prayer is public and in common; and when we pray, we pray not for ourselves alone, but for the whole people, because we the people are one. The God of peace and the Teacher of concord, who taught unity, willed that one should thus pray for all, even as he himself bore all of us alone."[92]

Obviously, Cyprian speaks of the community prayer in this passage. But this law applies not just to liturgical prayer since this law is part of the very structure of the Lord's prayer. Prayer in the secret of one's room (Matt 6:6) cannot be self-centered. Thus is verified what we wrote above: salvation always implies the others. For Christians, the subject of existence is no longer their ego-centered selves. They let go of their selves, "in Christ," even in their most personal actions. As a consequence, their lives are, in every aspect, flesh of the church because they are flesh of Christ.

---

[92] Cyprian, *On the Lord's Prayer,* 8.4-5, in Roberts, 8:403. See Ambrose, *Commentary on Cain and Abel* 1.9.34-39, in *Hexameron, Paradise, and Cain and Abel,* trans. John J. Savage, Fathers of the Church 42 (New York: Fathers of the Church, 1961) 390–95; Theodore of Mopsuestia, *Homily* 11.9, *Les Homélies catéchétiques de Théodore de Mopsueste,* trans. Raymond Tonneau and Robert Devresse, Studi e testi 145 (Rome: Vatican City, 1949) 299.

2. In virtue of its sacrificial nature, the church cannot be a servant of the world. It is the priest of the love of God in and for the world. Because the Spirit of the Lord Jesus, the priest of God, dwells in it, it offers "in Christ," in its life, the sacrifice of humanity to the glory of the Father. In this sacrifice are found all the components we have pondered over. It is not possible to confuse the church with a group simply following "the example of Christ," who would be its ethics teacher, having bequeathed to it norms of behavior.[93] It is, in the world and for eternity, infinitely more: it is the fruit produced in concrete life by the great letting go of self that the sacrifice of the Lord was and continues to be in his members, his branches, his priesthood and his "priestly house." Augustine would say that it is the sacrifice of Christ in that of Christians and the sacrifice of Christians in that of Christ. The nuance is clear. In the church, Christ communicates *himself* in his sacrifice of reconciliation and communion.

Such is the living flesh of the church. And it never ceases to celebrate this sacrifice "in the sacrament of the altar, known to the faithful, in which the church teaches that it itself is offered in the offering it makes to God," since it is the sacrament of its *communion, the sacrament of the flesh of Christ,* which becomes its own flesh.[94]

[93] What we have in mind is a rather widespread view of the church's mission reduced to a moralistic and pietistic scheme. This simplification is of course very old; it was held by many bishops of the Constantinian church and was opposed, as is well known, by Athanasius. Christ Jesus, he said, is more than a teacher of wisdom, more than an example: he is the presence and the gift of God's salvation. He is the Savior "communicating his own person to humankind." The Church is the place where this "communication" occurs.

[94] Augustine, *City of God* 10.6, in Schaff, 2:184. On the difficult question of sacrifice, see in particular Helmer Ringgren, *Sacrifice in the Bible* (London, 1962); de Vaux, *Sacrifices;* Robert J. Daly, *Christian Sacrifice: The Judaeo-Christian Background before Origen* (Washington, Catholic University, 1978); Tibor Horvath, *The Sacrificial Interpretation of Jesus' Achievement in the New Testament: Historical Development and Its Reasons* (New York: Philosophical Library, 1979); Frances Margaret Young, *The Use of Sacrificial Ideas in Greek Christian Writers from the New Testament to John Chrysostom,* Patristic Monograph Series 5 (Cambridge: Philadelphia Patristic Foundation, 1979); Jacques Vidal, "Sacrifice," in *Dictionnaire des religions,* ed. Paul Poupard (Paris: Presses Universitaires de France, 1984); Paul Lamarche, "Sacrifice," in *DSp* 1990.

Flesh of the Church, Flesh of Christ

We had proposed to demonstrate what the "flesh of the church" is: communion of life for humanity reconciled with the Father and with itself "in Christ." We have seen that through the power of the Spirit and the word, it is the "flesh of Christ" in the osmosis of the sacrificial flesh of the Lord and the concrete life of the baptized, a *circumincessio* (a true mutual inhabiting), of which the Eucharist is the sacrament.

1. Obviously, to speak of the "flesh of the church" is to refuse to see in it a purely invisible reality. But to link, as tradition does, this flesh to the risen body of the Lord given in the Eucharist is also to refuse to reduce the church of God to its visible reality.

To describe the "flesh of the church" as a network of relationships between brothers and sisters in which the individuals renounce their self-centeredness in the sacrifice of *agapē* which makes them, as Christians, inseparable from others, is to refuse to see the church as the sum or the juxtaposition of "justified" individuals. But to say that this communion is that of persons held in communion with the God and Father of Jesus Christ, a communion in which every person is called by her or his name (see Isa 49:1) in the Spirit, is also to refuse to reduce the church of God to a vast system of human solidarity and generosity; rather, it is to open a wide space to the personal encounter with the living God.

To declare that the pilgrim church is forever bonded with the ministry of the apostolic community by its hierarchical structure is to refuse to see in it a purely charismatic event without essential connection with history. But to underscore that this structure has no place in the eternal liturgy and that here on earth it is at the service of the grace of communion is also to refuse to limit the church to its hierarchical structure.

To hold that the reconciliation prescribed by the gospel is actualized in the geographical and cultural space called the local church is to refuse to make of the church a vague and abstract reality without concrete link to the places where men and women are born, work, live, suffer, take delight, love, express themselves, create history, and live on in their children. But to confess that at the eucharistic synaxis the church "which is in such and such a place" recognizes its communion with all the eucharistic communities scattered throughout the world, both with those which have existed since Pentecost and those which will exist until the Day of the Lord, and with the heavenly liturgy of the elect is also to refuse to enclose the church within the boundaries which fragment humankind; rather, it is to give to catholicity the amplitude of a reconciliation involving the whole creation in the communion of God.

This necessary symbiosis or communion between the visible and the invisible, the communal and the personal, the hierarchical and the charismatic (in the traditional meaning of the term), the local and the universal, enables us to perceive the nature of the church of God. According to Pascal's insight, it is—in the depth of communion created by the Spirit—the knot that ties these contrary things. Its riches reside there and manifest themselves in holiness, apostolicity, catholicity, and unity. This knot constitutes its being. It forms its flesh within the condition of sinful humanity.

It is the flesh of a community which in Christ and the Spirit reaches unto all the way to the invisible, the transcendent, the holy, the God and Father but also embraces what is human with its reality, its poverty, its frailty. It is the flesh of a community in which no one lives for oneself but for the Father, and lives for the Father only by letting go of oneself for the benefit of others, a letting go which is, however, a way of loving oneself (Mark 8:35; Matt 16:25; Luke 9:24). Inspired by Augustine, we spoke of *circumincessio* in *agapē*. Again, Pascal explains this with his usual genius:

"To be a member is to have neither life, being, nor movement except through the spirit of the body, and for the body.

"The separate member, seeing no longer the body to which it belongs, has only a perishing and dying existence. Yet it believes it is a whole, and seeing not the body on which it depends, it believes it depends only on self, and desires to make itself both centre and body. But not having in itself a principle of life, it only goes astray, and is astonished in the uncertainty of its being; perceiving in fact that it is not a body, and still not seeing that it is a member of a body. In short, when it comes to know itself, it has returned as it were to its own home, and loves itself only for the body. It deplores its past wanderings.

"It cannot by its nature love any other thing, except for itself and to subject it to self, because each thing loves itself more than all. But in loving the body, it loves itself, because it only exists in it, by it, and for it. *Qui adhaeret Deo unus spiritus est* [The one who loves God is one spirit with God (1 Cor 6:17)].

"The body loves the hand; and the hand, if it had a will, should love itself in the same way as it is loved by the soul. All love which goes beyond this is unfair.

"*Adhaerens Deo unus spiritus est*. We love ourselves, because we are members of Jesus Christ. We love Jesus Christ, because He is the body of which we are members. All is one, one is in the other, like the Three Persons."[1]

2. Because its flesh is flesh of mutual love unceasingly renewed by the Eucharist where the risen One makes it his own, Augustine said, and because this flesh is made up of the most concrete human realities, the church of God is, as it were, the healing of the body of wounded humanity. This is the church's fundamental contribution to the life and destiny of humanity.

Indeed, we must resist the temptation, reoccurring today, of reducing the church's place in the world to that of a preacher of ethics, an agent of philanthropic endeavors, a creator of magnanimous ideologies. The church is essentially the presence of a space in which the fabric of the "humanity-God-wants" is restored, an ideal for which men and women of today yearn, often without realizing it. In fact, the generous commitments to justice, freedom, equality of opportunity and rights remain incomplete, sometimes even ambiguous if an authentic, entirely gratuitous fellowship is not reestablished. The communion offered by the gospel is a desire, perhaps hidden or repressed, ineradicable from the human heart. Is this not visible even in the desire which attracts man to woman? When diversity and difference become division and

---

[1] Blaise Pascal, *Pensées*, no. 483, in *Pascal's Pensées*, trans. William F. Trotter (1923; reprint, New York: Dutton, 1958) 134.

selfish concentration on oneself, to the tearing apart of mutual love, then Scripture calls it the evil of humanity, a failure which spells wounds and pain, death and tears (see Rev 21:4). The church is grafted onto the great pain-ridden body of humankind. And the graft is but a fragment taken from the reconciling power of the cross.

It is here that what we have seen of the Christian sacrifice, which is precisely where this living flesh of mutual love and communion is restored, reveals its full scope. The church accomplishes what Philo already perceived to be the people of God's role as substitute by "[offering] up prayers and feasts and firstfruits on behalf of the whole human race . . . [for] others who have fled from the service they should have rendered."[2] And even its involvement in "the sacrifice of service to the poor" goes beyond mere social work. Whether in its liturgy, its social action, the private inner life of its faithful alone with God (to which certain people would want to limit the church's ultimate purpose), the church, which is the body of Christ, the vine of the Father, the "priestly house of the king," preserves alive for the good of humanity the mediational function fulfilled "once for all" (ephapax) by Christ Jesus. It is the flesh of Christ.

We must be correctly understood. We are not speaking of continued incarnation. One knows the most prudent way in which Lumen Gentium has made use of the "no mean analogy" by which the church is compared "to the mystery of the incarnate Word" (no. 8). Our perspective is different; it is that of the "in Christ," of communion (koinōnia). In a radical and absolute dependence, by which everything is gratuitously given to it by the Spirit, the church "receives" to make its own Christ's intercession, Christ's diakonia, Christ's word of teaching, with its frequent ethical implications, Christ's solitary struggle of Gethsemane preceded by nights of prayer in solitude (Matt 14:23; Luke 6:12; 11:1). In the human space and time in which it lives, every local church has for its mission to actualize this "once for all" of the intercession, service, teaching, and private prayer of the One it lives by and who lives in it; and it does this by taking into account the joys and pains, the projects and needs of its portion of humanity. As a consequence, its communion opens, "in Christ," onto the universality of mutual charity and the catholicity of salvation. In the local church, the silences and oversights, the refusals and deafness "proper to this specific place" are assumed before God into Christ's universal media-

---

[2] Philo, Special Laws 2.167, in Philo, Works, 584.

tion. In this again, it is the graft of the humanity-God-wants, the flesh of Christ, on the vast body of humanity.

3. Because it is a sacrifice to God, the church never ceases to receive itself from Christ "in the spirit." As Augustine understood by listening to the faith of the local churches, the heart of this "reception" is the Eucharist. Often, the West will be tempted to dislocate this relationship between word, Eucharist, and church of God. Following its instinct, the West will tend to see the church as a society of baptized persons held together by obedience to the word, rather than as the communion united by the eucharistic body. The West will not be insightful in its perception of the link between Holy Spirit and church. Whereas the great tradition of the undivided church, to which the East has remained faithful, sees in the sacrament (and especially the eucharistic synaxis) "the locus of the Spirit," the West has sometimes sought for the Holy Spirit in pseudo-sacramental activities. It will even happen that in the Latin Catholic Church, and not only in the Reformation, the unbreakable bond between church, Holy Spirit, and Eucharist will be forgotten.[3] However, what we have studied shows that when, in *Lumen Gentium*, the Roman Catholic Church affirms on several occasions the osmosis between Eucharist and church, it does no more than reprise its own tradition.[4] Number 26, one of the most important passages of

[3] We shall give only one example, an article on spirituality, not without quality in other respects, which one of our skeptical correspondents considers the "normal position" in the West "even after Vatican II": "Sept étapes sur la route de l'espérance," *Sources vives* 12 (1986) 53–58. One would expect to see the Eucharist figuring as a key-step since it is the Eucharist which feeds us with Christ's resurrection body. But it is mentioned in passing (one line) and only because it enables the baptized to grow to their full stature (p. 56). There is no hint of an ecclesial effect of the Eucharist nor of its link with the Spirit. The overall view is strictly individualistic, and the communal perspective appears—after a pause at purgatory—only with the mention of those who are "in the vision of glory." How is it possible to speak of "solitary" journey to God? To us, this seems foreign to the purest tradition.

[4] Thus, "In the sacrament of the Eucharistic bread, the unity of believers, who form one body in Christ (see 1 Cor 10:17), is both expressed and achieved" (no. 3, p. 3). "Really sharing in the body of the Lord in the breaking of the Eucharistic bread, we are taken up into communion with him and with one another" (no. 7, p. 7). "Strengthened by the body of Christ in the Eucharistic communion, they manifest in a concrete way that unity of God's people which this most holy sacrament aptly signifies and admirably realizes" (no. 11, p. 15). "In [the local churches] the faithful are gathered together by the preaching of the Gospel of Christ, and the mystery of the Lord's Supper is celebrated, 'so that, by means of the flesh and

the document, simply repeats the most ancient Western doctrine, to which in any case it explicitly refers in its quotations, taken from Augustine and Leo the Great through the channel of Thomas Aquinas:

"This church of Christ is really present in all legitimately organized local groups of the faithful which, united with their pastors, are also called churches in the New Testament. For these are in fact, in their own localities, the new people called by God, in the holy Spirit and with full conviction (see 1 Thess 1:5). In them the faithful are gathered together by the preaching of the Gospel of Christ, and the mystery of the Lord's Supper is celebrated 'so that, by means of the flesh and blood of the Lord the whole brotherhood and sisterhood of the body may be welded together.' In any community of the altar, under the sacred ministry of the bishop, a manifest symbol is to be seen of that charity and 'unity of the mystical body, without which there can be no salvation.' In these communities, though they may often be small and poor, or dispersed, Christ is present through whose power and influence the one, holy, catholic and apostolic church is constituted. For 'the sharing in the body and blood of Christ has no other effect than to accomplish our transformation into that which we receive.'"[5]

The fact that there is coincidence between this doctrine and that which the East has always professed proves that—without denying its own specific character—the Latin Church has understood the fundamental law of the return to communion. May each tradition renew its certitude at the very source from which it sprang. Unity does not result from a collage of confessional groups. On the contrary, it is the consequence of the reappearance of the same and indivisible apostolic source within the immense variety of communities which claim to belong to Christ Jesus. We have seen that the relation between Eucharist and church belongs to this apostolic fountainhead and how it gave rise to the same vision of the church's nature among all those whom

---

blood of the Lord, the whole brotherhood and sisterhood of the body may be welded together" [Mosarabic prayer, in *PL* 96:759B] (no. 26, pp. 36–37). "[Christ] is continually active in the world in order to lead people to the church and through it to join them more closely to himself; by nourishing them with his own body and blood, he makes them sharers in his glorious life" (no. 48, p. 72). Vatican Council II, *The Basic Sixteen Documents: Constitutions, Decrees, Declarations,* completely rev., trans. in incl. lang., ed. Austin Flannery (Northport, N.Y.: Costello, 1996).

[5] *Lumen Gentium,* no. 26, in ibid., 36–37.

we may consider the most eminent witnesses of the various ecclesial traditions during the patristic era. By reexamining itself in comparison with the apostolic source, Vatican II has caused the relation between Eucharist and church to be rediscovered; it had been lost sight of for several centuries in the West, where it was recognized only sporadically but without ever being denied. And thus, a bond of unity has been extended between Eastern and Western churches, which recognize themselves as sisters in the Eucharist.

4. The church receives itself from Christ in the Eucharist. But it receives itself thus in the Holy Spirit, through the apostles and then through the ordained ministry which reechoes in the diversity of places and the succession of times the "once for all" of the apostolic work. At the end of our study, it seems important to us to make clear the indispensable and essential function of this ministry in view of what we have found to be the "living flesh" of the church of God: by its very nature the church is a sacrifice offered to the glory of the God and Father of the Lord Jesus Christ; this nature is imprinted in the church by the eucharistic communion with the sacrifice of the Lord and with his flesh of reconciliation.

Since the apostles, since those whom they themselves chose to succeed them (in the transmissible part of their function as witnesses of the death-resurrection) and also those they selected as auxiliaries for the care of the communities born of their preaching, the ordained ministry has been an integral part of what we may call "the continual birthing of the church of God in the world." Of course, only Christ, together with the Spirit, causes the church to be born. Augustine's thought, which uses another biblical image, is well known:

"The Lord Jesus Christ builds his own house. Many toil in building, but unless he builds, 'those who build it labor in vain' [Ps 127:1]. Who are they who toil in building it? All who preach the word of God in the church, the ministers of God's mysteries. We are all running, we are all toiling, we are all building now, and others have run, toiled, and built before us. . . . We therefore speak without; he builds within. . . . He himself builds, he himself admonishes, he himself opens understanding, he himself kindles your understanding to lead you to faith; and yet, we still toil like laborers."[6]

---

[6] *Exp on Ps* 127.1, in Schaff, 8:606.

Why is the ministry, sustained by the Spirit of God, necessary since everything comes from Christ? Precisely in order to manifest that everything comes from Christ. The necessity for the ministry is not of the same order as the necessity for canonical laws and prescriptions which regulate the life of the community. The ministry is necessary because of the sacramental nature of the church, the sacrificial nature which constitutes the flesh of the church. The church must know, announce, manifest that only in Christ and through Christ can it be the sacrifice that pleases the Father in the world. For he alone has been and remains for eternity the perfect offering of humankind. The church is a sacrifice acceptable to the Father only because it is held in the embrace of Christ's sacrifice. We have shown this. The ordained minister—in virtue of an ordination invested with a responsibility that is much wider than he or she—is appointed to be a reminder to the church of this radical dependency at all times and in all its activities. The ordained minister is a sacrament of Christ inasmuch as Christ is the other by whom the community *as such* must be taught, served, nourished, comforted, guided, and, more fundamentally, given to itself in the Eucharist in order to become the "holy priestly community" offering "spiritual sacrifices acceptable to God through Jesus Christ" (1 Pet 2:5). It is a function characterized by both an extreme nobility and an extreme poverty. The tragedy is that too often the nobility is exalted and the poverty obfuscated. Sometimes people even define the church by its ministry whereas the ministry should be defined by its place within the church. In that case, the church of God is understood more as a society ruled by obedience to the hierarchy than as a communion in the "once for all" of the Lord's sacrifice. Such a church is a skeleton without flesh.

5. We think that we have studied in depth the nature of the communion which defines the church. This communion comes wholly from the sacrifice of Christ, described in Ephesians (see Eph 2:16) as the sacrifice of the reconciliation of humankind reunited into the one sacrifice to the glory of the Father. In it individuals are recreated and saved precisely because in the communion with Christ they are liberated, through grace, from the chains of their self-imprisonment preventing them from seeing the other except as serving their self-interest; they are freed from the straitjacket of humanity's madness which the Bible calls the sin of the world. In communion, individuals become persons:

"[In the early part of the last century], an Eskimo and an Ethiopian meet in the temperate zone and both at once exclaim: 'I am cold,' says the Ethiopian, 'give me your furs'; 'I am hot,' says the Eskimo, 'give me your feathers.' Each one has seen in the other the *thing* he needs, not the other human being who must also live (for in this case, each one would have surmised that the thing needed is also necessary to the other). In any case, the concern for one's own life would have restrained each one from a total commitment to the challenge. But the mutually profitable exchange has reassured them both, albeit without mutual love, albeit without either gaining the victory.—And society sees to it that an Eskimo always meets an Ethiopian and that in this way, its fragile children may receive, without having to fight for it, the soup they themselves *do not know how to prepare* and, once the soup is ready, *may know how to defend it against others.*"[7]

This parable betrays a rare perspicaciousness. Furthermore,

"if a person seeks refuge near the beloved, she or he will not be able to be satisfied: no kiss, no embrace, none of the demonstrations invented by love will enable them to melt into one another; on the contrary, they will still be two, and each one will stand alone and different before the other.

"Humans lament this solitude, but if they find it lamentable—it is because, *being themselves, they feel alone:* they do not feel *with anyone* and lack everything. . . .

"Humans hope that other things in the future will bring them what they feel they are lacking in themselves: *self-possession;* but inasmuch as they wish, inasmuch as they are preoccupied with the future, they *escape themselves in every present.*"[8]

The ecclesiology of communion does not say anything else, but it adds an answer: the gospel of God making possible the eucharistic union of sisters and brothers, a frail lighted space "in the night of solitudes."

Thus the Eucharist begins with the proclamation of the word. This word unveils the great plan of God, transmits the invitation of Christ:

[7] Carlo Michelstaedter, *La Persuasion et la Rhétorique* (Sommières: Éclat, 1989) 140–41. [Carlo Michelstaedter (d. 1910), *La persuasione e la rettorica,* ed. Sergio Campailla, Piccola biblioteca Adelphi 131 (reprint; Milan: Adelphi, 1982)].
   [8] Ibid., 43.

"If you knew the gift of God . . . " (John 4:10). The Eucharist is the source of the mission.

6. How can we avoid ending this study on a note of anxiety and sadness? At the same time the Catholic Church—strongly encouraged by the teaching of Vatican II—recovers the ecclesiology of communion and its emphasis on the Eucharist, it is shaken by a very grave crisis in the ordained ministry. For lack of ministers, the Eucharist is celebrated less and less. In certain regions, in comparison with the neighboring Anglican or Orthodox communities, the Catholic Church appears low church, that is to say, a church in which sacraments are no longer celebrated in their normal form, are even no longer the heart of community life. The establishment of Sunday services without Mass are the last resort, and communion with pre-consecrated hosts poses theological problems.

It would be tragic to see the Catholic Church come to the point of denying in its praxis what some observers of the ecumenical movement regard as one of its principal contributions to the rediscovery of the nature of ecclesial communion. Is not selling the Eucharist cut-rate selling the church of God cut-rate?

Subject Index

Scripture Index